COSTUMES
FOR PLAYS
AND PLAYING

COSTUMES
FOR PLAYS AND PLAYING

written and illustrated by

Gail E. Haley

METHUEN

New York   Toronto   London   Sydney   Wellington

ALSO by Gail E. Haley

A STORY, A STORY (winner of the Caldecott Medal)

JACK JOUETT'S RIDE

THE POST OFFICE CAT (winner of the Kate Greenaway Medal)

This edition published in the United States
by Methuen, Inc.

Printed and bound in the United States of America
78 79 80 81   1 2 3 4 5

Dedication

This book is dedicated to my mother and father
who first taught me the joys of costume-making
and made my first "horse."

Contents

You are what you pretend to be. So
be careful what you pretend to be.

Kurt Vonnegurt Jr.—**Mother Night**

 **Introduction**

A costume is a new skin. You become that person, animal or thing while you wear it. It allows you to feel what it was like to be an American Indian stalking deer or buffalo, a knight on a dragon hunt, a princess on her way to a ball, or Robin Hood leading his men from Sherwood Forest. A costume turns you into a magician who can create illusions of other times and places. It's also a present to people's eyes and imagination. A funny outfit makes them laugh. A frightening disguise can give them prickles down their spines. You'll include your family, friends, neighbors, or the audience at a school play in your world of make-believe. In order to achieve that you must get to know your character inside and out.

Try out several ideas or variations before starting to assemble or make your costume. Turn to page 130 of this book and experiment with exercises in make-believe. You'll be able to discover which role suits you best. The more thoroughly you research the character you choose to be, the more authentic he or she will turn out.

How to decide who or what you want to be

You can be anyone or anything you like if you use your imagination. Look in your school or public library for reference books to inspire you. Study the illustrations in books about history, fashions and travel. Collect pictures

from magazines, newspapers and travel brochures. Think about why a character that interests you looks or dresses as he does.

A knight's armor protected him from the sword blows of his enemies. The heavy, multi-layered gowns of kings, queens, lords and ladies of medieval days kept them warm in drafty, unheated castles. But an acrobat needs lightweight, skintight clothing that allows him to move freely. People's life styles and occupations are often reflected in their clothing. The peddler shown on the opposite page dates from Shakespeare's time. He had neither store nor warehouse. He carried all he owned and sold in a tray hung from his neck.

Every creature that burrows, climbs or flies is affected by its environment, by what protection it needs, and how it obtains its food. A yak is covered with shaggy fur since it lives in the bitter cold climate of the Himalayas. Elephants and hippopotami don't need fur in the tropical climates in which they live. A tiger's stripes blend in with bamboo, tall grasses and patterns of light and shade in the jungle. An anteater needs his long nose to burrow into ant hills. You must therefore try to find out as much as possible about any animal, person or make-believe creature you choose to be, before you begin making a costume.

It's fun to think about who does what and why; where people live and sleep; what they eat, and what sort of noises they make. You may want to invent an entirely imaginary creature. It could originate from a strange kingdom or another planet in outer space. Perhaps you'd like to be a "purple, squeaky, six-legged box-head!"

Designing your costume

The picture on this page shows a young man at the court of King Henry VII. The character you choose to be may differ, but the method of planning his or her costume should be the same as that shown here. You'll need a pair of scissors, a piece of thick construction paper or thin cardboard, onion skin or tracing paper, a soft pencil, and a ballpoint pen. You may wish to color your drawing with crayons or colored pencils.

1. Place the tracing paper over the outline figure on the opposite page. It represents you. Trace over the heavy black outlines, but not the dotted ones, with a soft pencil. Then turn the tracing paper over and place it, face down, onto the cardboard or construction paper. Redraw all lines that show through the tracing paper, pressing down hard with the ballpoint pen. The figure you traced will appear on the cardboard.

2. Now decide who or what you would like to be. Look through this book and whatever other reference material or pictures you have collected. Draw the front of your chosen costume over the figure traced on the cardboard. Design it so that it can be made later, full-size, to fit you, using paper, cloth, discarded clothing, papier mâché or whatever materials you have at hand. Draw details such as buttons, belts, laces, ruffles or fur on your sketch.

3. Cut out the costumed figure along the outside outlines of your sketch. Turn this cutout drawing face down on the table and draw the back view.

4. You can make a number of different sketches, trying out various ideas until you decide which character you want to be, and which costume to make and wear.

How to assemble parts of your costume

The reference books you study at home and in your school or public library should inspire you. Your exercises in make-believe will have helped you imagine what it might feel like inside the costume you plan to make. The drawings you made will have let you know how you'll look when your costume is finished. But the real fun starts with making the costume itself.

Decide on a base for your costume. Look for old and discarded clothing in your closets, rag bag or attic (see page 8). An old pair of green stockings could cover the legs of an alligator, a flower's stem, or Robin Hood's calves. A hooded sweater can be the base for a rabbit's suit or a Hobbit's costume.

You can also use everyday clothes as part of your costume. You'll find suggestions throughout this book for tying or buttoning accessories to good clothes without spoiling them for daily wear. They'll be as good as before once you remove added buttons or untie portions you added for your costume. The success of your costume does not depend on how much money you spend, but on your own ingenuity and invention.

Lay out all suitable ready-made or discarded clothing you can find. Ask yourself what else you might need or could use. Which cloth, paper or other remnants could provide accessories for your costume and make it look authentic? Study the index at the end of this book. Turn to pages 70-85 if you need to make a hat. See page 102 if your shoes need buckles. Or leaf through all the pages until you discover inspirations for whatever interests you. There are many different ways to make the same costume.

The Viking shown on this page is dressed in a pair of old pyjama pants laced round with rags, a sweat shirt, an old towel with a hole cut into it, and a belt. Discover how to make his helmet on page 66. Cloaks are described on page 50. And you can find out how to make shields on page 110.

✂ Three characters that show how to use this book

Witch. Her dress should be a nightgown or a pinned up adult dress. Refer to "Belts," (see page 34) to discover how to make her bodice. You can find out how to make her hat on pages 74-76. Masks (see page 86) or make-up (see page 94) will let you be as gruesome as you wish. This costume can be completed with a broom for flying and a pot for boiling horrendous potions.

Clown. Add collar and cuffs cut from a discarded shirt to any striped T-shirt. Get hold of a cast-off tie that hasn't been worn in years. Discover how to make the clown's suspenders (see page 13). Use a clean mop to improvise his wig (see page 98). Find out how to make funny noses and apply make-up (see pages 92-95). Turn to page 105 to discover how to make floppy shoes. Look among your own, or a brother's or sister's discarded toys for props. The more ridiculous they are, the better. A stuffed toy piglet, teddy bear, or elephant, carried under your arm, will complete your clown costume.

Rabbit. The bunny shown here is dressed in a sweater with a hood, a pair of pants, and sneakers. Rubber boots will do equally well. You can discover how to make whiskers on page 95. The rabbit's bow can be made out of an old belt or a wide ribbon. Animal ear-making is described on pages 36-38. Add a real carrot in case the rabbit gets hungry, and a basket for collecting or distributing Easter eggs. Don't forget the tail. See page 41 for details on how to make it.

✂ How to organize and use a treasure box

A large trunk or an old toy box can become a most useful dressing-up and costume accessory storage place. Mother's, aunt's and grandmother's discards and out-of-date clothing will help you fill it quickly. The more old-fashioned such articles are, the more useful and fun they can be for costume making. Add old evening dresses, worn-out pyjamas, nightgowns and slips, moth-eaten sweaters, old suits, old coats, tattered blankets, towels, sheets and curtains, worn-out and outgrown baby and children's clothes, and other interesting apparel that no one wants to wear any more, and that can't be given away or sold. Also keep costumes and fancy dresses you've made but no longer need or wear, or that have been discarded by other family members or friends. The more fabric, clothing, costume accessories and parts you collect, the easier it will be for you to dress up with your friends when they come to play. Such a collection is equally useful for school plays, church performances or masquerade parties.

Look round in secondhand clothing stores and at rummage sales for special articles of clothing, accessories, fur, belts or jewelry. They can often be had for a few pennies and they may be just what you've been looking for.

Keep an assortment of smaller boxes in your treasure chest. Use one for make-up, another for safety pins, buttons, ribbon remnants, binding, braid, or rug samples, beads and other pieces of costume jewelry or decorative materials that would otherwise be scattered among the larger items. Hats and other objects that crush easily should also be stored in separate boxes or containers.

Such a treasure box can provide many opportunities for improvisation. An old pair of stockings or an outgrown baby sweater can be turned into an excellent hat for a "jester." Try to think of amusing and ingenious ways to use what you have collected. Nothing need be what it is or was. Most of the adult clothing you collect will be too large. The following pages show how these can be altered to fit you. Evening gown straps can be pulled up and tied at the shoulder to become a dress that just reaches the floor for you. Old pants can be cut down to fit the length of your legs and stuffed with a pillow to fill them out.

✂ A costume wardrobe for dramatic and school plays

A costume wardrobe is simply a larger version of the treasure box. If you attend drama classes or plan a school play, such a wardrobe is essential. Accumulate discarded clothing in a closet or on a rack. Ask all members of your class and your friends to collect whatever articles and accessories might be useful, especially those described on pages 8 and 9. Make sure that all old clothing you collect is cleaned before use in costume making. New clothing, fabric, or costumes are expensive. So limit yourself to what you and your friends can find around your homes or collect from relatives and neighbors.

Members of your play or dramatic group can visit upholsterers, furniture, home decoration and hardware stores, furriers, printers, and manufacturers of all sorts in your community. Collect free scrap materials, samples and remnants made of paper, cardboard, fabric, plastic or foil.

The method described on pages 4 and 5 is as useful for planning a costume for a masquerade party as for a play to be performed at school or

elsewhere. Page 6 describes how to lay out the available materials. Dress up the play's cast in the available clothing and the bits and pieces in your wardrobe that come close to the character each is assigned to portray. Then pin up each garment and make the accessories from the cloth scraps, paper, foil or other materials, as suggested on the following pages. The special character of each part will grow in your own mind, and in that of each player, as the costumes take shape.

More ambitious productions may require a color-coordinated wardrobe. Then it is wisest to assign one member of the group to be wardrobe mistress or costume designer. A mother, teacher, or older sister can help if they own a sewing machine. But anyone can make costume alterations by hand, using staples, safety pins, adhesive tape, or paste, even when no sewing machine is available. Such costumes can withstand the wear and tear of one or two performances. Never throw anything away; large garments can be cut down, refitted, or cut up to make bodices, belts, hats and other apparel. Now leaf through the rest of this book and consult the index to discover how to create particular characters.

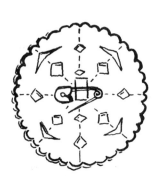

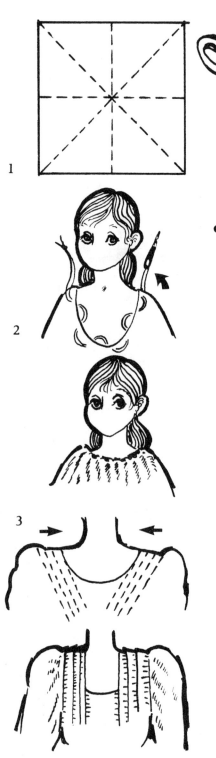

1

2

3

✂ Adapting old clothes, discarded fabrics and other materials

Safety pins are the quickest means for making alterations on existing garments. Pin them **inside** tucks and hems where they cannot be seen. When this is not possible, use a fancy, decorative pin or brooch to make the required alterations on the outside of the gown or suit. Or, a safety pin can be covered with an ornament you have made out of paper, foil or cloth, and then used in the same manner.

1. Fold a square of fabric or paper along diagonals as shown. Then, using a pair of scissors, cut shapes into the folded edges. Tape, glue, or sew the finished design onto the stationary side of the safety pin. A whole costume can be designed in this manner.

2. If the **neckline** of an existing garment is too large, thread a needle with strong thread and gather the open edge of the collar. Pull up on the thread until the neckline fits comfortably and then secure the end of the thread by knotting or sewing it into the cloth.

3. If **shoulders** of shirt or jacket are too wide, pleat them carefully until they fit. If several pleats are required it's best to sew them in with needle and thread. A single pleat or fold can be fastened with a fancy pin, button, or cloth rosette (see 1 above).

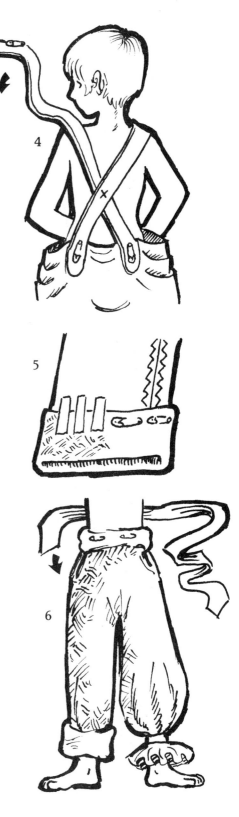

4. **Loose skirts or pants** can be held up by suspenders if these are available. You can make suspenders with ribbon or drapery tape and four safety pins, as shown in the accompanying illustration. Measure the distance from the front skirt or pant waistline, over the shoulders to the waistline in back. Cut two pieces of ribbon or tape to the required length. Attach the suspenders to the garment's waist front and back and, if you wish, sew the tapes together where they cross, for permanence. Cover the suspenders with a belted, long top or shirt.

5. There are many ways to **alter pants**, depending on the fabric and the kind of costume you choose to make. To shorten pants that are too long in the legs, cut them to the required length with pinking shears or scissors, or tuck the cuffs under. Pin tucked-under pant legs with safety pins, secure them with masking tape, or leave the ragged edges exposed, depending on the desired effect.

6. If **too high and full** at the midriff, long pants and skirts can be rolled over at the waist, or pinned or stapled if required. Cover the rolled bulk of fabric at the waistline with a wide belt or sash made out of an old tie. A clown's or Turk's baggy pants should be gathered at the ankles with ribbon, string or elastic. Let them blouse at the knees. For a baggy, Charlie Chaplin costume, just roll up the bottoms to achieve the desired result.

Knee breeches are useful for a large variety of costumes. They are as appropriate for pirates chiefs as for seventeenth and eighteenth century gentlemen. The principle is the same, whether they are pantaloons for a circus performer or for a nineteen-thirties golfer's plus-fours. Any old pair of pants, woolen underwear or discarded heavy stockings can be used. The fabric of the pants should, of course, be appropriate to the character of the costume. See page 13 for instructions on how to alter the waist.

a) To convert pants into pantaloons or breeches, cut the legs at an angle as shown, with the long, tapered end facing out.
b) The cut will look like a long triangle from the side. Cut through the middle of this triangle up to just below the knee.
c) Roll up the legs until they reach just below the knees.
d) Then tie the two ends of each legging as shown. Sew a bright button over the knot to hide it and for decoration.

Ordinary or flared blue jeans make good pants for sailors and pirates. Faded jeans are useful for peasant, itinerant worker, early American settler or revolutionary army costumes. Striped pyjama or satin pants are adaptable for Portuguese or Spanish explorer costumes. Dancers' leotards can be used as pants for gentlemen representing a variety of historic periods. Army pants are easily painted, or they can be decorated with magic markers. Other sew and iron-on decorative ideas are suggested throughout this book.

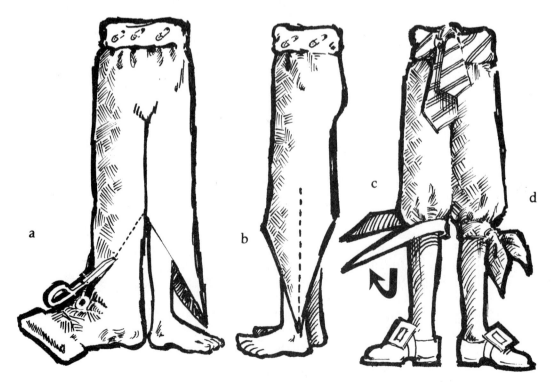

See pages 102-109 for ideas on how to make a variety of footwear that matches pants of any period or style.

Ruffled shirts require an adult's old shirt as a base.

a) Turn the collar over and tuck it inside as shown. Then put the shirt on backwards.

b) If the shirt is a discard and won't be used again for normal wear, cut off a few inches from the shirt tail to make ruffles. Or use a discarded, ruffled curtain, old lace, or a lace-edged handkerchief and sew or pin it to the front of the shirt with a brooch or safety pin. Tuck the shirt in at the waist and let it blouse slightly.

c) Turn up the sleeves at the cuffs.

d) Pin or resew the button on the outside as shown. The excess material can be used to form a ruffled cuff, or a separate ruffle or piece of lace can be added.

A ruffled shirt can be worn for a variety of different costumes. Long bloused shirts were fashionable during many centuries. Worn with ordinary pants or leotards, a ruffled shirt will turn you into a court jester or a fourteenth century gentleman. See pages 34-35 for ideas on how to make belts. Each different kind will help turn a ruffled shirt into a costume for a different period. Pins, ties and scarves at the throat of the shirt can create yet other transformations.

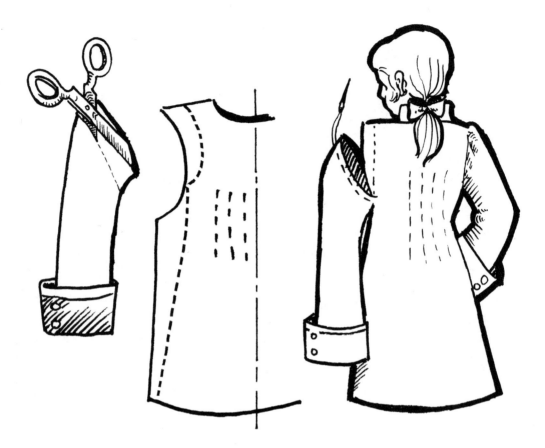

✂ Adapting old clothes, discarded fabrics and other materials *(continued)*

Jacket or frock coat. Cut out the sleeves at the armhole seams from any old jacket. Ask for mother's help if necessary. A new seam must then be sewn from the armhole to the tail of the garment. Next, cut the sleeve down to size. Turn up the sleeve at the wrists if cuffs are required. Gather the fabric at the top of the sleeve until it fits the new armhole. Sew the sleeve in. Cover ragged seams with fancy binding or velvet ribbon. Keep in mind that, seen from a distance, as in a stage performance, small irregularities in sewing or binding won't be noticed by the audience.

New pockets, lapels and cuffs can be cut from contrasting fabric, felt, or paper, and sewn or adhered to the costume. To form a narrow waist, sew darts into the back of the jacket, as shown.

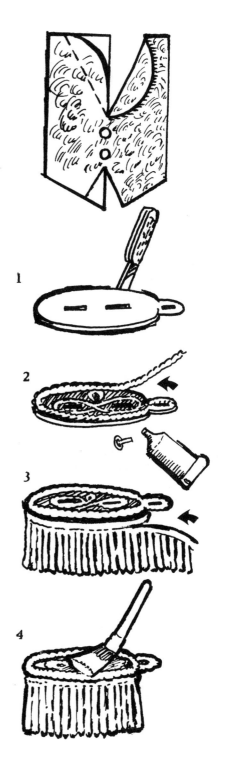

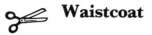 Waistcoat

Any old shirt, sweater or blouse can be cut down to make a waistcoat. Scraps of fabric or fancy materials can be laid out, fitted, and cut as shown, to make a "false" one. Pin it in place under the jacket. Fancy buttons can be pinned or sewn to it, as required.

✄ Epaulettes

Army and naval officers' dress uniforms of the past indicated rank by shoulder boards called "epaulettes." They can be made in the following manner:

1. Cut a piece of cardboard into two oval or rectangular shapes, including slits long and wide enough to allow button to pass through. The same buttons must be sewn to the costume's shoulders leaving the thread loose enough for buttoning. Be sure to measure the epaulettes' size so that they fit the wearer's shoulders. Double the cardboard shapes and glue them together for strength, one set for each shoulder.
2. Glue designs made with string or twine to the top surface of each epaulette.
3. Paste or glue braid, looped string, or fringe round the edges.
4. Paint the epaulettes, including braid or string designs, with gold or silver paint (see pages 112-113).

Button the epaulettes to the shoulders of the uniform, or sew or tie them on with gold-painted string, colored wool, or braid.

✂ Early American costume

Use the methods described on page 12 to draw up neckline and sleeves of any old, discarded, long-sleeved dress or nightgown. If the skirt is much too long, gather it up and stitch or pin at the waist, indicated in the diagram by a dotted line, to form a puff or bustle. Cut collar and cuffs out of stiff paper or cardboard, or stiff or starched fabric, or use any that might be available from a discarded garment. For a matching, gathered hat, see page 78. Any shawl or apron will complete the costume.

✂ 17th or 18th century lady's costume

Try to find a discarded, polished chintz or cotton gown, an old evening dress, a tattered curtain or bedspread. Any existing garment can be used and adapted, with sleeves, collar, bustle and shawl added, if the fabric is strong enough. As for any costume making, it's always best to start with a base garment, adding to it by pinning, stapling, or sewing dress details to it. Or, if only parts for a costume are available, these can be assembled and sewn or pinned together to form the whole.

Either is simpler than starting to design and sew a whole new costume out of a piece of fabric. The diagrams on this page show how different costume parts can be taken from existing garments, improvised and assembled. See pages 30-33 for suggestions concerning buttoned-on or tied-on sleeves. Pages 70-81 show how to make a variety of hats; wigmaking is described on pages 98-99; shoe buckles are shown on pages 102-103; and ideas for make-up to complete the disguise can be found on pages 92-95.

   Don't just copy the examples shown on these and other pages of this book. Experiment, improvise, change and alter what is described and illustrated, using whatever actual materials, remnants and garment parts are available to you. Adapt what you have and use the ideas shown here merely as points of departure for your own inventions and costume design.

✂ Costumes that button

The people shown on these pages lived in different centuries and in different places. At all times and everywhere, clothing was made out of whatever material was available. In some periods rank dictated color, material, and style. In making your costumes you will have to use whatever you can find or make in order to create the illusion or character you wish to represent.

1. **Lady at the court of King Richard II.** She wore fine, handwoven linens or wool, trimmed perhaps with fur. You can improvise her overdress by cutting down a discarded adult gown, a curtain, or an old blanket. A nightgown, sweater, or a long shirt can be worn underneath.

2. **A New Zealand, Maori warrior.** He wears a cloak made of pigeon feathers. Any fake fur, discarded bathmat, dyed chenille, or wooly fabric can be turned into a cloak that looks credible. Borrow a skirt from one of the family or a friend, or see page 46 for instructions on how to make a wrapped skirt, or "pagne."

3. **Cavalier of the reign of King William III.** This costume can be created by cutting down an adult coat (see page 16). Pages 72-75 give directions for making a three-cornered hat. His curls can be made of an old wig, or colored wool attached directly to the hat. Knee breeches are described on page 14. Improvise the pieces of brocade at the cuffs, belt, and

down the front of the waistcoat, using discarded remnants of fancy fabric, or design, cut out, and glue crumpled foil or doilies to these various costume parts.

4. **17th century lady's hunting dress.** Such a gown matches that of the cavalier, described in 3. above. It can be designed in a similar manner. Use a real feather or, if none is available, make your own out of paper (see page 58), or fringed cloth. Cuffs, dress borders, and the laced shirt front can be pinned or stitched onto an ordinary, everyday dress or a fitted nighty or coat. See page 96 for suggestions about improvising the hairdo.

5. **Gentlemen in the reign of King Henry IV.** Use one of your mother's old dresses and cut the hem into scallops. Sleeves can be made out of an old pillow case. Add upholstery braid as shown, or cut scallops out of foil or paper. See page 73 for ideas on how to make the hat. Use any available fancy belt, or make one as described on pages 34-35.

6. **Lady in the reign of King Edward II.** With a little imagination this costume can be created from almost any available scrap materials. Decide just how you want the finished costume to look. Any length of fabric can be pinned or stitched to a nighty or discarded adult dress. Cowl and head dress can be made out of cardboard or papier mâché (see pages 66-69). Draped curtain material, netting, or a silk scarf wound around the hat completes this costume.

Aprons, bustles, overskirts

A bibbed apron tied over any girl's dress turns her into Alice in Wonderland. If such an apron is not available, it can be rapidly sewn by anyone familiar with simple stitches. A plain, white apron that ties round the waist can be adapted by adding a bib, shoulder straps, ruffles, if desired, and buttons. For one-time wear or a single performance, a bibbed apron can be made out of crepe paper. Such an apron, customarily worn by housewives, servants and even ladies of fashion in preceding centuries, gives any garment an old-fashioned look. It also hides unfinished, pinned, stapled or taped-together portions of a costume.

1. **To make an overskirt,** gather a knee-length piece of fabric, and attach a waistband at the top edge.

2. Turn the fabric over onto the wrong side. Turn up the waistband and sew in place as shown. Stuff dry leaves, hay, tissue or crumpled paper into the shape that results.

3. Gather up the sides, as indicated by dotted lines on the diagram, and secure them, as shown, with bows.

4. **A bustle** can be made by sewing a long rectangle of cloth to a waist band. Gather up along the dotted lines. Secure the gathered material on the underside. Stuff with newspaper, tissue paper or leaves.

5. Tie the bustle in front or wrap ties around and secure in back.

✂ Military coats and uniforms

An officer's coat can be made by adding a flared skirt to any sweater or sweat shirt. Both should be of the same color or, if they are not, they can be dyed to match. See page 124 for suggestions on how to dye fabric.

It's best to make a newspaper pattern (see pages 52-53) before cutting out the skirt, peplum or tail for a uniform coat. When the paper shape looks right and fits, pin the fabric to it and, after adding a little along the seams if the costume is to be sewn, cut out the fabric shape. It can then be decorated with braid, trim, rope, felt, paper or magic markers.

Sew or pin the skirt to the sweater. Add paper or stiff fabric collar and cuffs, brass or painted cardboard buttons. Consult books about military uniforms of different periods for details that enable you to add authentic touches. Sashes, belts, and bandoliers, appropriate to different armies and periods, can be made as detailed on pages 17 and 34.

A military frock coat can be made in much the same manner as the skirted one, using a sweater, jacket or woolen shirt as the base and adding tails.

Experiment with different ways to attach the tails. They can be buttoned round the waist, or sewn or buttoned to the basic garment. Consider how often the costume is to be worn, how much rough usage it must withstand, and whether the basic garment is needed again for daily wear.

Tails can be made out of stiff fabric, felt, canvas, brocade, or heavy wool cloth cut from an old suit or blanket. Stiffener, bought in sheets at any store selling sewing notions, can be ironed onto the back of lighter weight fabrics. Or a wire frame, feather boning, or cardboard can be glued, stapled or stitched to the fabric to give it shape, weight and stiffness.

If the military frock coat's flaps or tails are to be turned back, they can be lined with different colored fabric and buttoned or hooked back to the outside of the costume's skirt, as shown in diagrams 1 and 2.

✂ Collars and cuffs

Any addition of collars and cuffs to rag bag or everyday clothing, converts it instantly into a costume. A handkerchief, scarf, tie or shawl, if appropriate to the character to be represented, serves similar purposes. The following are a few examples of typical collars and cuffs and how to make them.

1. **Elizabethan stand-up collar** can be cut from starched fabric, netting, wallpaper, or a textured plastic place mat. Or an old piece of lace can be ironed to stiff inner facing, or glued to cardboard, and then cut out in the shape shown. A large paper doily will serve equally well.

2. **The sailor's collar** can be cut out of an old bedsheet and lined or colored with a laundry marker or fabric paint. The collar can be edged with binding, for permanence.

3. **Pilgrim Father or Peter Pan collar** can be cut out of felt or stiff paper. Use a paper hole punch to punch holes at the corners at which it is to be tied and lace or knot ribbon or string

through them. Use the same shape, technique and materials to make matching cuffs.

4. **Stand-up collar** made of cloth or felt can be stiffened with plastic or cardboard strips (see shaded lines inside diagram). Sew on hooks and eyes as shown. Such a collar is extremely versatile and can be adapted to a large variety of costumes, periods and styles.

a. A ruffle or lace edging, added to top and bottom of the collar shown in diagram 4, or an added brooch or pin changes its character entirely.

b. A scarf, ruffle, braid or stars pasted or sewn to the collar shown in diagram 4 turns it into a civilian or military dress accessory.

c. Feathers, paper cut-out scales, sequins, fake fur and other textured materials turn a stand-up collar into the neck for any animal costume. Worn with a sweater, blouse or leotards such a collar transforms you into any real or make-believe creature.

d. Gather a ribbon of fabric to top of collar, or experiment with other variations appropriate to your costume.

✂ Ruffs and ruffled collars

Ruffs and ruffled collars are essential accessories for clown and jester costumes. But they are also part of male and female garments worn at many different periods in history. They are quite simple to make, though they seem complicated. The most useful materials for making ruffs and ruffled collars are netting, fine cotton, crisp curtain material, inner facing (but not the kind used for "ironing-on"), paper tablecloths, disposable cleaning towels, or crepe paper. Starched material, like fabric cut from an old bedsheet, can also be used, as can wide satin ribbon used for gift wrapping.

1. Sew pieces of any of the stiff material suggested into a continuous ribbon long enough to encircle your neck at least four times. Thread a large needle with strong twine or string and knot the ends. Except when satin ribbon is used, fold the sewn-together length of fabric in half. Make the first stitch at one end of the fold, running the needle in and out through the material as shown. Push the fabric towards the sewn end after each four or five stitches have been made, in order to gather it.

2. After stitching to the end of the folded ribbon (or the unfolded ribbon if satin ribbon is used), adjust the gathered material to fit your neckline. Then make a knot to secure the gathering. Pieces of ribbon sewn over the knotted string ends will hide them from view. If soft fabric is used to make the ruff, two can be made and worn, one above the other.

3. More complicated period ruffs merely require smaller stitches at the open edge of the gathered ruff and, possibly, small beads sewn along the ends where pleats meet, as shown.

Experiment with different pleats and fabrics. Use several layers of material. If stiff fabric is used, line the inside of the ruff with soft ribbon or binding to avoid rubbing at the neck. This is specially important if paper is used. Shape the paper so that it does not cut into your chin. Paper ruffs can also be made out of accordion-folded party decorations that can be bought at novelty and notion counters. Glue a ribbon or length of soft cloth inside the shaped paper ruff to prevent rubbing and to help keep its shape.

Fasten the ends of the ruff with hook and eye, or with a button and loop. Or lengths of ribbon can be tied to the knotted ends of the string used to gether the ruff, by which to fasten the ruff round the neck. The knot can be hidden under a pin, and worn at front or back.

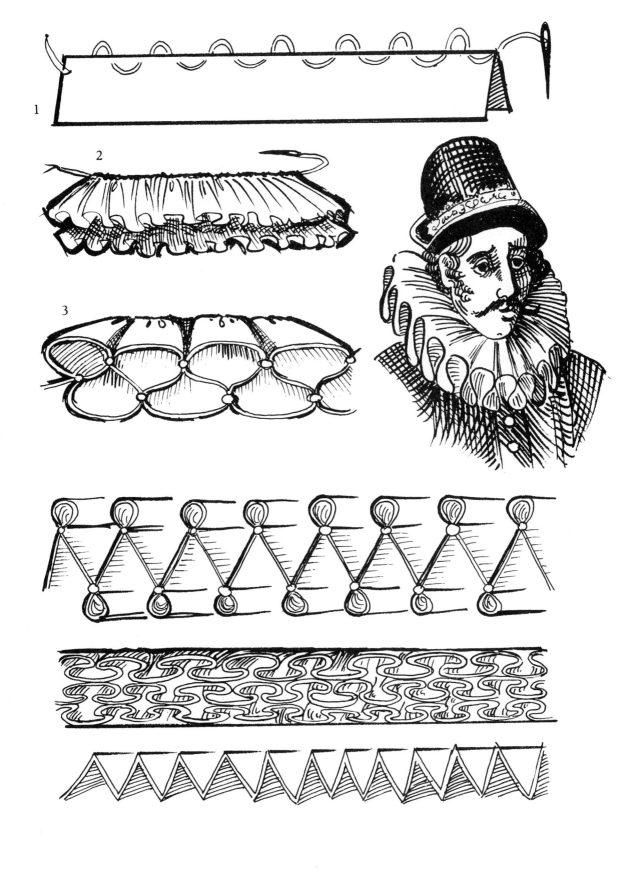

1

2

3

✂ Sleeves

The illustration on the left, top of page, shows a lady from the court of King François I of France. A professional costume designer might match her gown exactly. But the brocade would cost a great deal of money and the dress require professional sewing by a tailor or dressmaker.

The drawing on the right shows how this costume can be improvised with an ordinary sweater to which button-on sleeves, a ruffled collar and cuffs have been added. Look through your rag bag and pick out cloth remnants or a sample of upholstery fabric with which to fashion the sleeves. When cut out and sewn, they can be buttoned to the shoulders of the sweater. A second and third button may be required on each shoulder to keep the sleeves in place if heavy fabric is used. Additional strips of colored cloth or ribbon can be added to simulate decorative details.

1. Cut sleeves from an adult shirt. Gather, staple or sew the fabric in layers from top to bottom to achieve the effect shown. Use a piece of ribbon, or binding tape, for extra stability, and to fashion a loop for buttoning.
2. This is the basic, flattened-out pattern for an ordinary, long sleeve. Dotted lines Y and Z are the distance from armpit to wrist. Dot-dash line M, N is the distance from top of shoulder M to wrist YNZ. Add loop of ribbon or binding tape at M for buttoning. After cutting this shape out of fabric, turn it to the "wrong" side and sew, staple or tape edge Y to Z.

3. Turn the sewn sleeve inside out, so that the "right" side of the fabric faces out.

4. Now sew the large, top opening of the sleeve with a strong thread all round. Gather the fabric until this top opening fits the armhole of the sweater or other garment to which it is to be attached. Be sure to knot or sew the end of the thread into the fabric so that the gathering will not come undone. The sleeve can then be attached to the sweater with buttons, as described above. A ribbon or decorative border sewn round the gathering of the sleeve at the shoulder and at the wrists, will hide any irregularities.

Sleeves look prettier and more professional when sewn by machine. But for a party or theatrical costume they are quite as effective when sewn by hand, taped together or stapled. Save all leftover fancy fabric scraps. They can be used for other decorative detail.

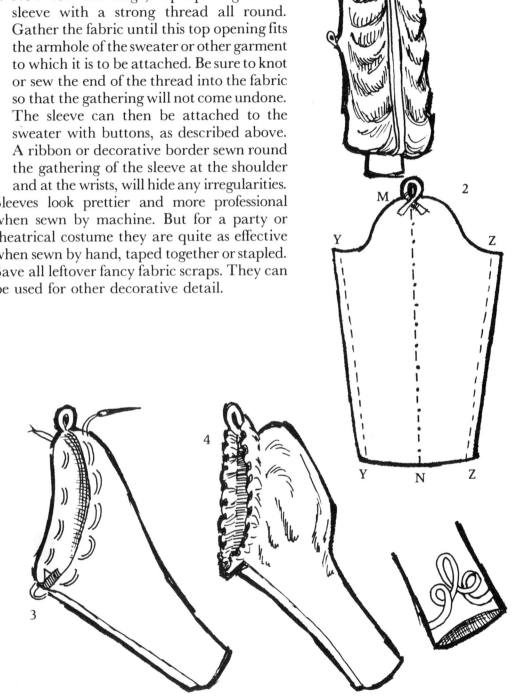

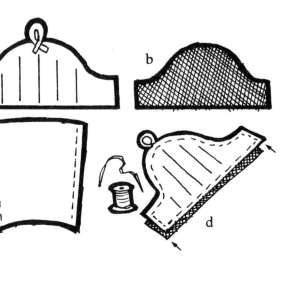

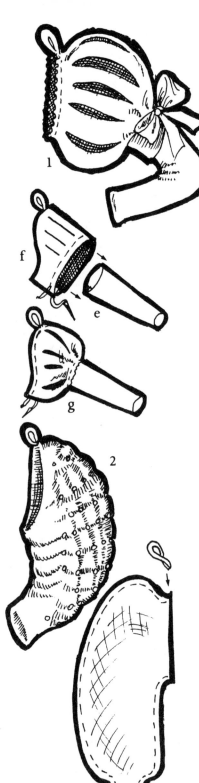

Sleeves *continued (see page 31, diags. 2, 3 and 4)*

1. **Slashed medieval sleeve.** Cut shapes (a), (b) and (c) out of fabric scraps or drapery samples. Shapes (a) and (c) should be cut from the same fabric. Shape (b) should be cut from fabric of a contrasting color. The slashes cut into shape (a) need not be finished. In period costumes they were left unhemmed. But if you wish to keep the edges of the slashes from unraveling, cut them with pinking shears or paint their edges with clear nail polish, liquid glue, or spray them with liquid starch.

Sew shape (a) to (b) along the dotted lines shown on diagram (d). Then sew the long sides of shape (c) together, wrong side out, to form the tubular sleeve. Turn this sleeve right side out when finished (see diagram (e)). Gather the straight opening of diagram (f). Sew gathered side to the largest opening of sewn together shape (e). They will then form the whole sleeve shown in diagram (g). Add ribbon over seam as shown in diagram (1). Button the finished sleeve to the basic costume, engaging a button sewn to the shoulder of the garment with the loop attached to the top of each sleeve.

2. **Medieval sleeve.** Such a sleeve is best cut from an old quilt or bedspread, as shown in pattern (a), and sewn together along the dotted lines on both long sides. As always, sew on the wrong side of the fabric, and turn to the right side when sewn. Sew on the button loop as indicated by the small arrow. Button the finished sleeve to the shoulder of a sweater or other garment. It can be worn equally well over a full coat or dressing gown, keeping you warm on a drafty stage.

3. **Flowing sleeve**
a. Draw the shape of your arm from shoulder to wrist on paper or cardboard as described on pages 52-53. Then draw the sleeve you need for your costume with crayon or felt marker. The dotted line indicates the shape of the shoulder and upper arm. Cut out the shape you have drawn.
b. Place the cut-out pattern on a folded piece of fabric. The row of arrows shows the fold. Pin the pattern all around as indicated and cut out the cloth shape, leaving the fold intact.
c. Sew the buttonhole loop at the shoulder point. Turn the fabric to the wrong side and sew the long, straight sides together as indicated by the dotted line. Turn to the right side, decorate and button onto the costume.

4. **Japanese sleeve.** Draw a pattern as in (3a) above. Allow a long panel to hang from wrist as shown. Transfer, cut, and sew as in (3). Sew along the dotted line as indicated. If desired, line the sleeve with fabric of a different color. Add a cuff if appropriate. To find out how to paint suitable designs on sleeves and costume turn to page 129.

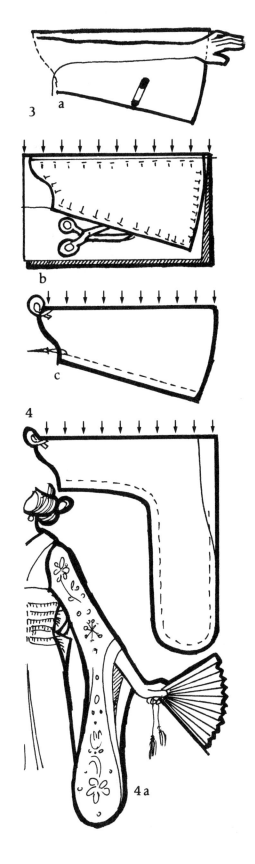

✂ Belts, bodices and stomachers

Decorative waistbands can be cut out of fancy fabric samples or scraps, felt, old clothing, paper or lightweight cardboard. They are essential accessories for many costumes from different periods. They also disguise clumsy alterations at the waist of existing garments. For Viking, Assyrian and similar draped costumes, belts and waistbands help define the contours of ordinary curtain materials, bedsheets or toweling used for period costumes. Measure your waist before laying out the pattern, and allow for overlap and seams.

1. **Bodice for milkmaid or lady.** Cut the shape shown out of stiff, black material, after measuring the waist to be fitted with tape measure or string. Punch holes along the short edges and lace through these with ribbon, felt or leather thong, heavy wool, or shoelaces.

2. **Egyptian draped belt.** Similar belts were worn in other cultures and times. Drape a decorative hanging over the buckle of an ordinary belt. Make the hanging out of painted cloth, paper or cardboard. Paste cut-out or add iron-on shapes to plain material cut to the desired shape.

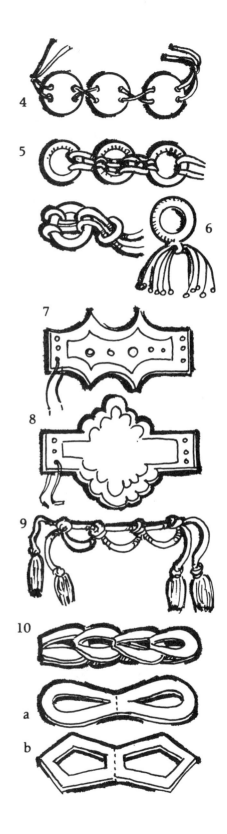

3. **King's stomacher.** Cut out the pattern from canvas or felt. Punch holes as shown and lace in back. The stomacher can be decorated with plastic lids or bottle caps stuck to it and painted gold or silver, with buttons pasted or sewn to the belt, or with colored paper or foil cut into disks and other decorative shapes.

4. **Disk belt.** Use plastic lids or painted and decorated cardboard disks. Punch holes into each disk as shown and lace one to the next, using as many as required to fit round the waist.

5. **Curtain ring belt.** Curtain rings or any rings cut out of construction paper or light cardboard can be laced together with doubled felt, leather thong, or twine to form a belt of any length.

6. **Tassle belt.** Tassles can be knotted into each of the curtain rings shown in 5 above, before lacing them together.

7. and 8. **Stomachers.** In addition to that shown in diagram 3 on the opposite page, a variety of different stomachers can be cut out of felt, canvas or foil-covered cardboard, and laced front and back. They can be painted, appliquéd, or have iron-on fabric stuck to them.

9. **Looped belt.** A doubled length of twine, curtain tie-back, rope or gold cord can be knotted at intervals to form this and similar belts. If you know macramé or knot-tying, you can invent any number of variations.

10. **Doubled, looped belt.** Cut out multiples of the shapes shown in (a), (b), or others from lightweight cardboard, felt, canvas or any stiff fabric. Fold and slip each through both loops of the next doubled link, until the required length is reached. The first and last links should be tied with cord, stapled or pasted together so that the whole belt can't separate. Then fasten the two ends of the belt at front or back of the garment with twine or a decorative pin or buckle.

✂ Button-on ears, masks, and tails

Animal costumes are easy to improvise and make. Start with any hooded sweater and leotards, pyjamas, or woolen underwear. Gloves, mittens or a pair of heavy woolen socks can be used as paws. For realism, all these can be dyed in the same color to approximate the color of skin or fur of the animal to be represented (see page 124 for dyeing information). An alligator naturally needs to be green; a cat, yellow, black or striped; a rabbit, white or brown; and a bird, blue or multicolored. A uniformly dyed assembly of such clothing, to which ears, tail, beak, mask, or wings are buttoned, can be extremely convincing and effective.

Button-on accessories can be made out of paper, cardboard, cloth, toweling, corduroy, foam rubber, felt, plush or fake fur. Most are available as remnants or in short lengths in stores. The basic shapes for different animal tails, ears and other identifying features are shown on the following pages. Sew buttons to appropriate places on ordinary clothing and attach the various costume parts. After use as a fancy dress or play costume, the buttons can be cut off and the clothing worn as before.

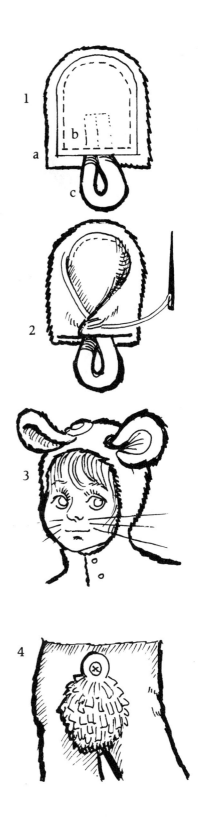

1. **Animal ears** are best lined with slightly smaller pieces of pink fabric sewn to the wrong side of the animal's fur. Once sewn together, turn the ear right side out, using the eraser end of a pencil. The furry edge of the ear will then show realistically round the pink, inside portion. (a) is the basic, button-on ear shape cut from plush, toweling, fake fur, or dyed fabric scraps. (b) is the pattern for the slightly smaller, matching pink fabric shape that defines the inside of the button-on ear. (c) is the loop with which the finished ear is attached to a button sewn to one or another side of the hood of the basic garment that is to be worn. These loops should be made out of identical fabric to that used for (a).

2. Fold and sew the bottom corners of the ear with a few stitches as shown.

3. Sew buttons on both sides of the hood of the sweater or other garment that is to be used, and button the finished ears to them.

4. Any matching **tail** can be attached to pyjama or other pants with a button sewn to the seat. See pages 40-41 for patterns and ideas for tails of different animals, all of which can be attached in this same manner.

✂ **Button-on ears, masks and tails** *(continued)*

1, 2 & 4. Different animals have different kinds of ears. Some stand up straight from the head. Others flop over. Those shown here are all "stand-up" ears. Each can be constructed out of two pieces of felt or cloth, as described in the text that accompanies diagrams 1 to 3 on the previous two pages, but with cut-out shapes of stiff paper or cardboard sandwiched between them to assure that they stand away from the head. Diagram 1 shows the pattern for a rabbit's ears. It should match the color of the hood and clothing to which it is to be attached. The same pattern can be used, in a gray colored fabric, for a donkey's ears. Diagram 4 shows the pattern for a cat's ear. Due to the relatively large size of a cat's ears in proportion to the size of its head, three buttons are needed to keep each in place.

Diagram 3 is a pattern for a dog's floppy ear. Diagram 3a shows how it should be attached to the costume hood.

Button-on masks. Masks, beaks, and visors can be made and buttoned to a hooded garment, in the same manner as button-on ears. Stiff paper or felt, glued or pasted to paper, are the most easily worked materials. Diagram 5 shows how wire or pipe cleaner can be sewed on underside of duck's bill for extra strength. The pictures below show some of the possibilities. Experiment with these ideas and with variations that may occur to you. The materials can be cut, folded or bent to approximate the contours of any human or animal head or feature, and then buttoned to the headgear. See pages 86-91 for other ways to make convincing masks out of paper, papier mâché, felt and cloth.

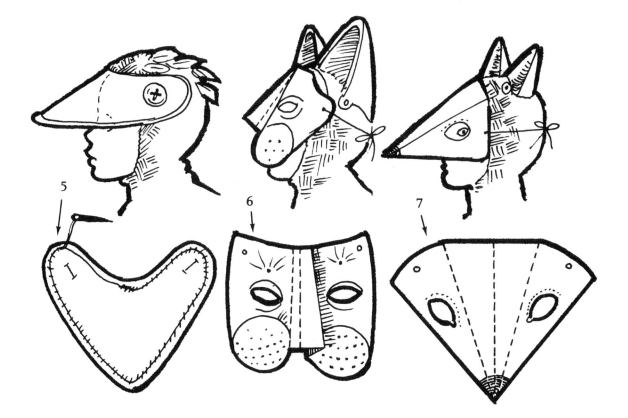

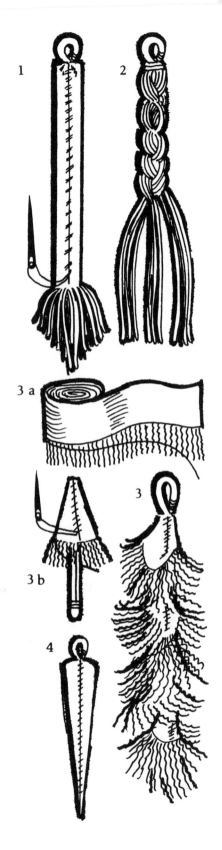

Button-on tails

The tails shown on this and on the opposite page belong to a variety of different species. They can be adapted to fit any animal, including many that are not mentioned. It's a good idea to make the loop, by which each tail is attached to the seat of the pants, out of elastic, to avoid possible tears in the fabric.

1. **Tufted tail.** Cut a strip out of plush, toweling, felt, or similar stiff cloth, three times as wide as the finished dimension required. Fold both edges until they meet in the center of the strip, and sew them on the underside, as shown. Stuff the inside of the tube thus made with cotton batting or shredded paper. Add a tuft of wool to one end and the elastic loop to the other, and then button the tail to the seat of the pants.

2. **Braided tail.** Measure and cut three bunches of wool, rags, or rope, each approximately forty-five cm (18″) long. Braid them as shown. Sew elastic loop to the top of the tail and button it to the garment.

3. **Fluffy tail.** Cut a strip of cloth, a meter (40″) or so long and about ten cm (4″) wide. Unravel about five cm (2″) of thread on one of the two long sides of the cloth strip. Roll the fringed strip into a tight coil as shown in (a). Push a pencil through the center of the coil (see diagram (b)) to form a spiral of cloth. Use a needle and thread to sew a few stitches and hold the spiral in place. Then extrude the spiral further and further, securing it with additional stitches until it is fully extended as shown in diagram 3. Once securely sewn, attach the elastic loop as shown.

4. **Stuffed tail.** Cut the fabric into a wide triangle. Fold the long sides so that they meet in the center on the underside. Sew them

together as shown in diagram (4), and stuff with cotton batting or shredded paper. This is a useful tail for a kangaroo, "Nut-Cracker Suite" rat, or perhaps a dragon.

The following are stiff, stick-out tails that must be sewn on the costume:

5. **Wire base.** Use copper or coat hanger wire. Make three loops at one end with a pair of pliers and twist the remaining wire into a single strand. Cover the straight, twisted wire strand with adhesive surgical, masking, or insulating tape, as shown. When completed, bend the three loops at the end at right angles to the straight, twisted wire and sew the loops to the seat of the costume pants.

6. **Feather tail.** Real feathers and others made of paper, cloth, or felt can be glued or secured with fine wire or tape to the looped wire base, as shown in diagram 5.

7. **Flowing horse's tail.** Use rope, twine, string, synthetic fibers, raffia, or heavy wool. Knot, tape or sew strands securely to a wire base, similar to but longer than that described.

8. **Rabbit's tail.** Use a ready made pom-pom, or wrap wool round a book as shown in (a). Then tie a piece of heavy string or wool through the loops along spine of the book and gather and tie them together tightly. Cut strands along open edge of the book as shown in diagram (b). When the wool is removed from the book it will form a fluffy, many-layered tail that can be sewn to the seat of the costume pants.

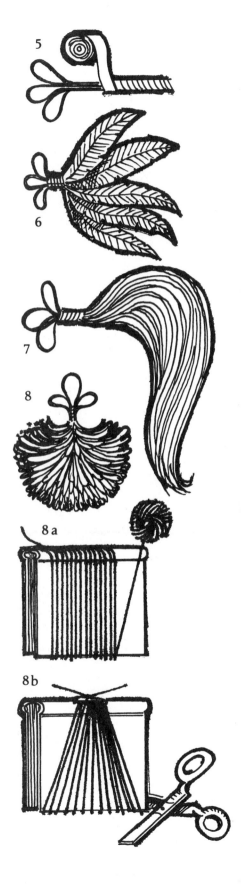

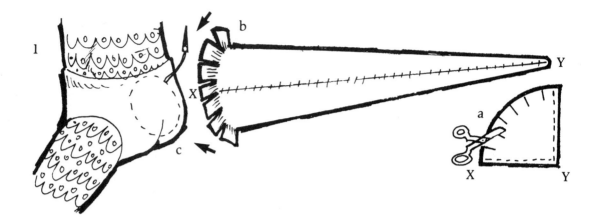

✂ Large tails

1. Wear a pair of swimming trunks over leotards, heavy stockings or woolen underwear. Heavy tails require a solid base to which they can be sewn or buttoned. It's best to make a newspaper or wrapping-paper pattern before cutting the cloth. Cut a pie-shaped segment out of paper, as shown in diagram (a). You'll then be able to make the required adaptations before pinning the paper pattern to the cloth for cutting. X, Y indicates seam in both diagrams (a) and (b).

Once you've established the actual dimensions of the tail, and have cut it out of paper, pin the paper to the cloth and add six mm (¼″) to both sides beyond the dotted lines to allow for the seam. Cut the cloth out according to the pattern and sew the long edges along the seam on the wrong side of the fabric, forming the shape shown in diagram (b). Now turn the tail right side out. The tabs shown along the wide base of the cone allow the tail to be sewn to the swimming trunks or other costume pants (see diagram (c)). Stuff the tail with cotton batting, cloth scraps, or crumpled newspaper. Then sew the tail firmly to the costume. Scales, fur or other details can be cut out of colored paper and pasted to the tail, painted or drawn on with magic markers.

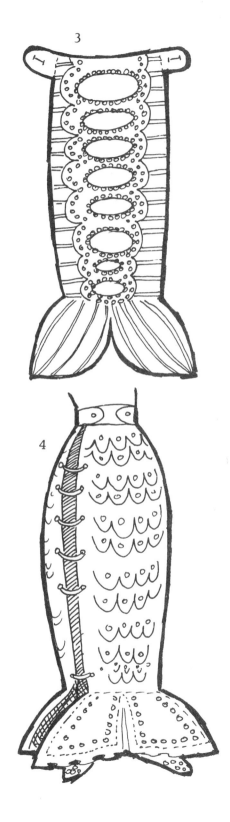

2. **Articulated tail.** Such a tail is good for "swishing." Staple cardboard rectangles or squares to both sides of a shaped cloth or canvas tail. Paint or decorate the cardboard with paper, glitter or sequins.

3. **Lobster tail.** Cut red cloth in the shape shown, long enough to reach from the waist to the floor. Glue or paste red paper, cardboard or foil shapes to the cloth and draw in details with a black laundry marker. Sew "button-on" tabs to the tail as shown on the diagram and button to the sides or front of waistband. Wear with red leotards, pants or woolen underwear.

4. **Fish or mermaid tail.** Cut front and back pattern out of green or blue fabric. Either incorporate the tail fins into the pattern or cut and sew them on separately. Decorate the fish tail by drawing scales, drawn with fabric marker, or by pasting glitter onto the cloth. Scales can also be cut out of colored paper or cloth and glued to the fabric in overlapping rows. If the tail needs to be stiff or rigid, wire or boning can be stitched or glued to the cloth. Use pieces of elastic down the sides to hold them together. Button to waistband of leotards or swimming trunks.

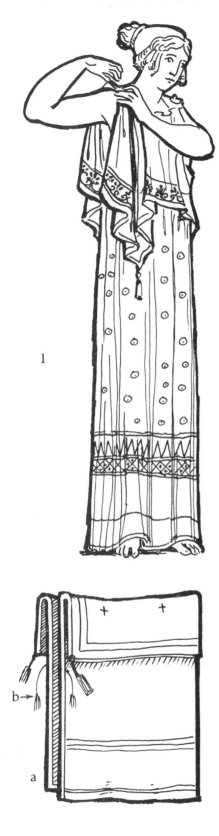

✂ Draping and folding

Long before the skills of cutting, shaping and sewing were known, clothing was draped in shapes based on the length of linen specially woven for wear. Study Greek vases, statues and engravings of Greco-Roman and earlier periods for costume and decorative details. Jewelry and other accessories are easy to improvise out of cardboard, string, wire and other materials (see pages 112-115). Page 107 shows how to make sandals appropriate to the periods when such gowns were worn. To make the costumes shown on this and the following pages, use fabric that drapes easily — an old bedsheet, sheer curtain material, or a length of muslin. Border designs can be made with black or brown laundry markers. Practice draping before wearing costume. Use extra pins if necessary.

1. **Greco-Roman chiton.** Fold a rectangle of cloth in half, and then fold the top over once more, as shown in (a), so that the distance from fold to floor is exactly the same as the distance from your shoulder to the floor. Use a safety pin to fasten the garment at point marked "x" on diagram (a), at both shoulders. You may wish to pin or sew the open side of the garment to facilitate wear. Or attach ties or ribbons as indicated by (b).

2. **Man's or boy's exomis.** Made of a shorter, smaller rectangle of cloth than the chiton described in 1. Fold the fabric in half. Pin the open side to one shoulder at (x) and allow the remaining fabric to drape loosely on the other side, leaving one shoulder bare. Use a belt made of cord or other material for wear round the waist (see pages 34-35). The skirt of this garment can be sewn on the side opening (y) if wished.

3. Chiton. Similar to that described in 1, except that it is belted and is not folded over at the top. Pin at both points marked (x) and tie at the waist with cord or sash (see pages 34-35). The belt helps shape and drape this garment and allows for blousing of the fabric below the arms.

4. Girl's peplos. Fold the fabric as in 1. To achieve the effect shown here, the fold should be less deep than that shown in 1.

The fold-over in 1 reaches to the waist. The fold-over in diagram 4 stops above the waist. Use a ribbon or piece of cord for belt. If desired, tuck an extra scarf or rectangle around waist as shown in 4.

✂ The pagne

1. From the days of ancient Greece to today in Africa and in the South Sea Islands, a floor length, wrapped skirt has signified the wearer's station in life and his authority. Family and tribal elders, chiefs and kings use the pagne as their official gown. Choose a length of material long enough to reach from waist to ankles, as shown in diagram 1, and wide enough to wrap round your body at least three times.

(a) and (b) show how to fold and wrap the garment round the waist. Attach point (x) to (x) with a safety pin for convenience. Pleat the remaining width of cloth as shown and tuck the top of the pleat into the waist to cover the safety pin, as shown in (b). Wear this costume with jewelry (see pages 112-115), a head dress (see pages 83-85), or make-up (see pages 92-95), depending on the geographic region or historic period to be represented.

To make a pagne appropriate to a period or region, choose a patterned fabric, or draw designs onto plain fabric to match that culture. Large designs and patterns in one color are typical of those used by South Sea islanders. African tribes often used striped fabric.

✂ The sari

The sari is worn by women and girls throughout India, Burma, Sri Lanka, Indochina and, in historic times, was the female attire among Persians. The fineness of the material used and its decorations indicate whether the wearer is of high rank or a commoner.

Use the sheerest material you can find — netting, curtain material or any other — to form and drape the sari. For one that is to be worn repeatedly, use a sheer synthetic. Decorate the border of the fabric with gold and silver painted designs and stripes, with glitter, or with gold and silver thread embroidery, foil, or sequins, to accentuate the edges. Be sure that paint or glue is dry before wearing the costume.

The sari is usually worn over a short-sleeved bodice and slim skirt. These can be dyed, together with the fabric for the sari, in the same or contrasting dye baths (see page 124) before they are decorated. Try to approximate the clothing shown in diagram 1 as closely as possible. An old vest or T-shirt can be cut down and adapted for the bodice. A discarded halfslip will do for the skirt.

To wear the sari, tuck or pin the fabric at the back of the waist as shown in (a). Bring the remaining fabric round to the front, up over your chest, and around the left shoulder. Let the rest of the cloth hang over your arm, facing to the rear as shown in (b).

Oriental women and girls wear a great deal of jewelry. They use ornaments for ears, arms, ankles and round the neck (see pages 112-115). Look at pictures and reproductions of miniatures of oriental, Indian and Persian life, artifacts, craft and jewelry. Much of the jewelry and many accessories are actually made out of papier mâché (see pages 62-69), sometimes inlaid with mirrors and foil.

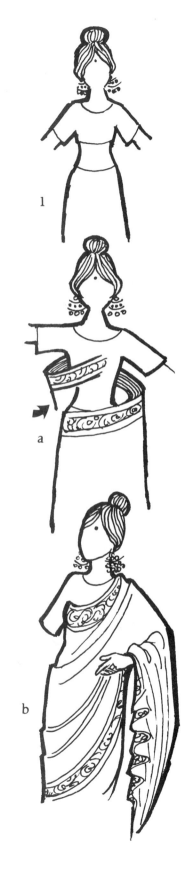

✂ The loincloth

American Indians, African tribesmen, Samurai warriors of Japan, East Indians, Pacific islanders and countless other people of the past and present have worn and still wear loincloths, sometimes as their only garment, and at other times as underwear. Egyptians, Abyssinians and Cretans in ancient times wore a skirt over a loincloth, as shown in diagrams (f) and (g).

To make a loincloth, the first requirement is a rawhide or other leather thong, twine, rope or sash (see diagram (b)), tied round the waist with the knot to one side. Choose a length of fabric as wide as your body, equal in length to the distance from your shoulder to the ground (see diagram (a)). Any cloth, toweling, or fake fur will do. Straddle the length of fabric and tuck front and back over the waistband from inside to outside, so that it is firm, though comfortable when you move about (see diagram (c)), The extra cloth is left hanging over the thong or cord front and back (see diagram (d)). Fasten the fabric to the cord with safety pins all around. Now untie the knotted sash or belt and, after removing the loincloth, make a few stitches in the fabric where it is folded over the cord to keep it from slipping (see diagram (e)). Designs that symbolize region, period or culture can be painted, embroidered, or adhered to the front and back flaps of the loincloth (see diagram (a)).

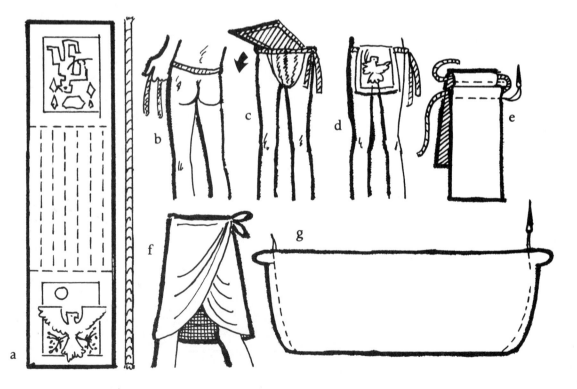

✂ Roman toga or African wrapped garment

In ancient Rome a toga was the mark of citizenship. No foreigner was allowed to wear one. Slaves, travelers and ambassadors of other nations were instantly recognized by their foreign clothing. The length, size, color and decoration of the toga indicated the rank of the wearer. This garment consisted of a semi-circle of material tucked in under one shoulder, and flowing loosely over the other (see diagram 1).

The African senator's robe (see diagram 2) is draped in the same manner. His toga is made out of a rectangular piece of fabric. Tuck one corner of this toga under one arm, pin at X as shown in diagram 1, and then wind it round, draping the cloth over shoulder and arm as shown in diagram 2. African dignitaries still wear a similar garment today. While the Roman toga was predominantly white or purple, the African version varies in design. Some are painted or dyed in different colors, others are printed or striped. African chiefs usually carry fly switches. You can make one out of raffia, nylon or yarn, taped to a short wooden or bamboo handle. See pages 112-115 for details on how to make Roman and African jewelry and accessories.

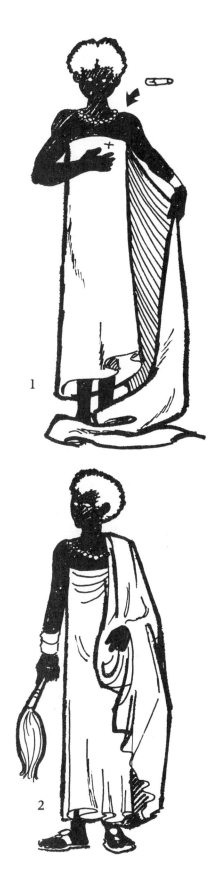

1

2

1

2

3

✂ Cloaks and capes

A cloak or cape tends to dramatize any costume for which one is appropriate. It lends an aura of mystery and, in some characters, danger to the part. It is easy to make and will keep you warm. This can be important on a drafty stage. Diagrams 1 to 5 show the basic shapes; how they are cut, gathered, fastened and worn; and how to drape them.

Old blankets, bedspreads, curtain material, or any other length of heavy fabric is suitable. You can also make a patchwork cape if sufficient sample swatches of upholstery or drapery fabric are available, sewn together at random. Fastenings at the throat can consist of old frogs, buttons, twine, drapery pulls, bits of chain from a hardware store, or nylon cord. Decorate the borders with sequins or glitter, or designs cut out of colored paper or foil, and glue them to the fabric. Iron-ons can also be effective.

1. A simple, gathered cape, suitable for a Robin Hood costume, among others. Turn over three or four cm (1½″) of one edge of the fabric. Insert a drawstring and sew along the dotted line, as shown. Then pull up on the string, gathering the hemmed edge of the cape and tie it round the neck as shown. In a play involving armies or different groups of people, costuming each side in different colored cloaks makes it easy to distinguish between them. Emblems and devices, made out of cloth or paper and pasted to cloaks, also help to identify particular characters.

2. **Medieval or opera cape.** An old blanket can be cut as shown to make this cape that overlaps in front.

3. A different version of the cape shown in 2, fastened at the throat.

4. **Open cape,** worn by Assyrian or Roman overseers. It is held in place at the throat by a cord or lightweight chain.

5. **Egyptian cape** that is cut away from the chest, leaving the undergarment exposed and permitting freedom of movement. Use classic Egyptian motifs on the collar. They can be appliquéd, adhered with iron-ons, or glued directly to the fabric, after the cape is designed and cut. Or they can be drawn on with fabric markers, or painted on with fabric paints.

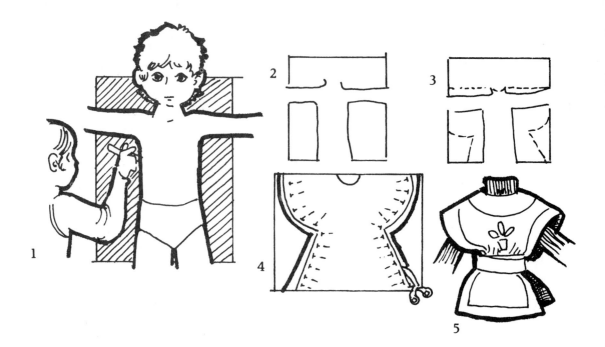

✂ Pattern-making

Making a paper pattern before cutting cloth saves a great deal of time and material. This may seem like taking an unnecessary extra step. But the longest way round is sometimes the shortest route to success when you set out to make costumes or accessories from scratch.

1. and 2. Newspaper sheets are the best and cheapest material for making costume patterns. Large sheets of brown or white wrapping paper can be even more useful. Also required are a fat felt marker or soft crayon and masking tape. Lie down on the flattened or taped-together paper and have a friend draw around the part of your body that the costume must fit.

3. Add extra dimensions to allow for body bulk and curvature, as well as for portions that come round the sides, or over and under the shoulders, arms or legs, and for seams. If several pieces must be cut and fitted — front, back, sides, or V-shaped inserts to allow for contours or movement — cut these out of the paper as well, and tape or pin them together or against the clothing you wear. Cut, fold under, and adapt these various paper shapes until they fit when assembled.

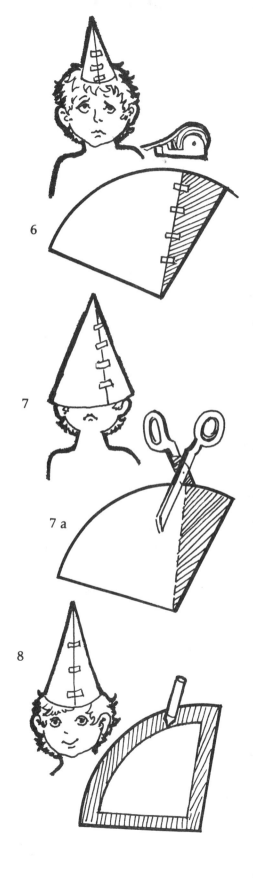

4. Unpin the finished patterns and take them apart, once you are satisfied. Separate all individual pieces and lay them out flat. These shapes must now be pinned to and cut out of cloth or other final material.

5. Sew, glue, or tape shapes together to form the finished garment. This same principle works for all clothing, hats, shoes, gloves, or any other garment that must fit you. Be sure to allow at least six mm (¼″) extra at all seams that are to be sewn, or twelve mm (½″) for edges that are to be glued.

6. and 7. If, after cutting the paper shapes, some prove too small, add and tape on additional paper pieces (the shaded area in diagram 6) until they fit. If the pattern is too large (see diagram 7) cut off small portions (see diagram 7(a)) until it fits.

When satisfied that the paper pattern is right, tape or trace it exactly onto foil, cardboard, leather, or any other final material you have selected. If the costume or accessory is to be made out of cloth, pin the paper pattern to the cloth with closely spaced straight pins (see diagram 4) after both the pattern and the fabric have been smoothed so that they are entirely wrinkle-free.

6

7

7 a

8

– 53 –

 **Paper costumes**

Paper costumes are easy to make. Paper is less expensive than cloth, though it is not a substitute. Paper costumes don't last as long as those made out of fabric, but they offer unique opportunities for fitting and design. Keep in mind that paper has sharp edges which can cut you. Aside from this, paper offers unlimited opportunities for costume-making. It can be taped, slotted or pasted together, painted, and decorated in countless ways. Consider some of the ingenious paper uses traditional in Japan. There people build houses, furnishings, lanterns and kites most successfully out of paper.

All costumes shown on both these pages can be made out of paper or paper products. Costumes made of other materials can be decorated with paper, foil and tissue. Corrugated cardboard can be curved round the body or round body parts. Left natural it looks like tree bark. When painted silver

it makes convincing armor. The papier mâché dividers used to prevent fruit from bruising in their crates, egg cartons, and similar paper products make excellent breast plates, shields, hats, jewelry, and other costume parts.

Paper can be painted with poster paints or acrylics. If poster colors are used, it's best to shellac or varnish the painted surfaces before the costume is worn, or else the colors may run. Finally, because of the stiffness of paper and cardboard, either may rub unless cloth undergarments are worn. Use pieces of foam rubber or wadded cloth under cardboard portions of costumes that might otherwise be uncomfortable.

Details about these and other ideas on how to use paper, cardboard, and papier mâché are described on the following pages. Don't just copy them. Use these as inspirations and improvise your own variations and innovations.

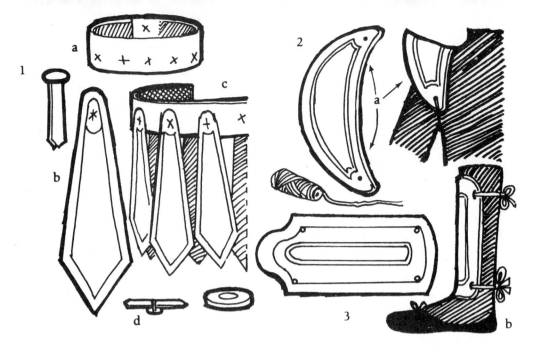

✂ Paper costumes — armor, greaves and ornaments

1. **Paper battle skirt.** Greeks, Romans and many medieval knights wore skirts made of leather, chain mail, or plated brass strips. These gave them protection, while allowing them movement on foot and on horseback. One version consists of a wide belt (a), from which arrow-shaped modules (b) are hung as shown in (c). The belt can be made out of cardboard, canvas, or other heavy cloth. Allow for overlap at back. Punch evenly spaced holes onto the belt, all round, using a hole punch. Design the shapes to be hung from the belt so that they reach just above the knees, and that they almost touch, when hung, at their widest bottom parts. Make one trial shape and trace as many others as required onto lightweight cardboard or stiff paper. Punch a hole into the top of each and fasten them to the holes made in the belt with paper fasteners, as shown in (d).

Cardboard modules can be decorated with magic marker or poster paint, before being hung. Don't bend the flanges of the paper fasteners back too far, or the hanging armor modules won't move freely. Cover the paper fastener flanges with fancy buttons, cork, or foil or silver-painted cardboard disks.

2. **Shoulder armor.** Similar shapes are suitable for both a knight's armor and for a spaceman's zero-gravity suit. Cut a crescent shape out of lightweight cardboard, large enough to cover the shoulder, the pointed ends reaching almost to the armpit. Punch holes into the two points of the crescent (a). Attach string or elastic to these holes. Make it long enough so that the shoulder armor can be tied under the arm. It can also be pinned with a safety pin, from underneath, or buttoned to the shoulder of the costume.

3. **Greaves.** Leg armor can be made out of cardboard in a variety of shapes. Cut and punch holes into the cardboard as shown. Attach elastic or string to each of the four holes and tie round the leg as shown in (b).

4. **Arm and leg bracelets.** These are not only useful for making armor, but the same basic design applies to any kind of arm or leg jewelry. The basic shape is shown in (a). It can be varied, scalloped and designed in a great many different ways along the top and bottom curved sides (see (b) and (c)). Work out the design on paper before transferring it to cardboard. Such bracelets can be taped or tied to arm or leg, after they have been painted or covered with foil.

5. **Headdress.** This basic shape also has a great many different applications, from Indian chief to emperor. Design and cut out the shape, or any variation, shown in (a), attach string or elastic to the holes, and tie loosely to the head after decorating it (b). The hanging shape, shown in (c), can be attached to the headdress with a paper fastener (see 1 on opposite page).

Fireproofing paper and cardboard

Paper or cardboard can be fire-retarded by brushing or wiping the following solution onto it with a sponge or rag. Saturate the paper well. Wipe off any excess and allow to dry. If paper or cardboard curl, either can be dried between two layers of newspaper weighted with telephone directories or other heavy books. Or they can be ironed between sheets of blotting paper after they have dried. Mix the ingredients listed below thoroughly in a large pot or plastic bowl.
NOTE: Sulphate of ammonia can be bought at any garden supply store; boric acid and borax at drug stores. Do not fireproof colored paper. It fades when moistened. Also be sure to wear rubber gloves while mixing and applying the mixture, and keep it from contact with skin and eyes.

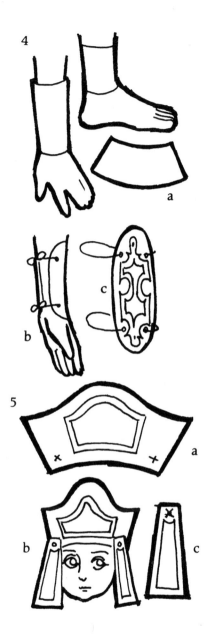

Solution:

Sulphate of ammonia	— 220 g
Boric acid crystals	— 84 g
Borax	— 56 g
Water	— 2½ liters (2½ qts)

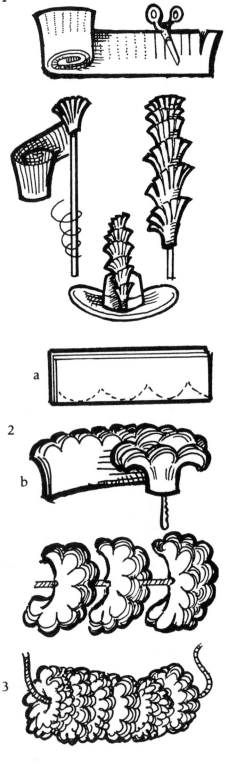

1. **Paper plume.** Cut a long ribbon of tissue paper, crepe paper, or newspaper. Make scissor cuts along one long side of this ribbon, at regular intervals as shown in (a). Glue or tape one end of this paper ribbon to a pipe cleaner or drinking straw, as shown in (b). When the glue has dried, spread paste along the entire length of the uncut side of the paper ribbon and then paste it, in a downward spiral, to the straw or pipe cleaner stem. Turn it over when the glue has dried and bend the paper strips outward to form the plume shown in (c). It's a useful hat or costume decoration, or a fly switch for an African chief.

2. **Paper rosettes.** Accordion pleat tissue or crepe paper into a tight stack and cut scallops along one edge, as shown in (a). Cover the straight unscalloped edge of the paper strip with paste and roll it tightly round a hairpin (see (b)). Hold in place with string or an elastic band until the paste is dry. Bend the leaves of the rosette outward and paste the bottom onto a hat or other costume part, as needed.

3. **Paper garland.** Make rosettes, as described in 2. Tie a burnt matchstick or button to one end of a piece of heavy twine and string the rosettes, one after another, all facing in the same direction.

Decorating large paper areas

Large sheets of paper used for paper costumes can be made dimensional and decorated in a variety of ways. See also pages 120-121 for ideas on how to make paper costumes out of paper bags. The following applies to such paper bag costumes as well.

Paper can be painted with poster colors, acrylics, or decorated with crayons and magic markers. Cut semicircles or points into paper and lift up tabs to form fish scales or feathers.

4. **Dimensional paper glueing.** Draw equidistant lines onto a sheet of large paper to be used in costume-making. Then cut as many strips of paper as long as the larger sheet is wide, each twice as wide as the distance between the lines, and as many such strips as the number of lines marked on the paper. Cut designs into the bottom edge of each strip, decorate it, curl it, or draw or paint designs onto it. Diagrams (a), (b), (c) and (d), show typical cuts and designs. Strip (c) shows a fringed, curled design that, when pasted down with other strips, gives a furry effect. Paper can be curled with fingers, or by drawing it firmly in one direction between dull scissor blade and ball of thumb. Strip (d) shows interior spaces cut out, with tufts of colored yarn tied to each loop.

Once a sufficient number of strips have been prepared, glue each top edge along one of the lines marked on the large sheet of paper. Start from the bottom of the sheet to achieve the overlapping effect shown in diagram 4.

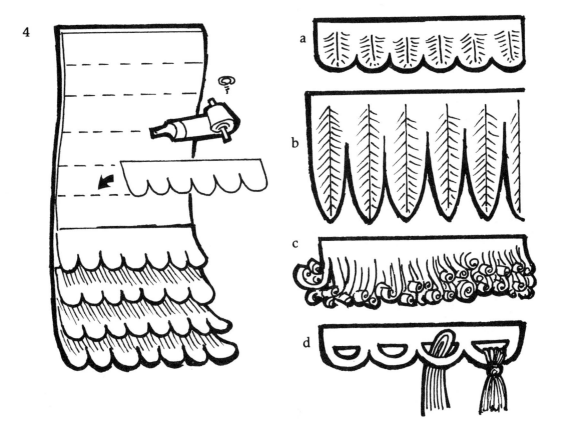

✂ Newspaper hat and sword

Equip yourself for a mock battle, in which no one can get hurt, with a paper soldier's hat that fits anyone, and a paper sword. You need several large sheets of newspaper, scissors and tape. Just follow these step-by-step instructions.

1. Hat

a. Use two large sheets of newspaper (not tabloid size). Stack them neatly and fold them together where they normally crease at the center fold. Then fold in half once more along the dotted line as shown, and make a sharp crease.

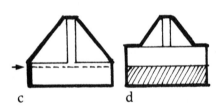

b. Fold the top right and left corners down along the dotted lines as shown, forming two triangles, and leaving about 4 cm (1½″) space between them.

c. Fold the top layer of the remaining bottom flap up over the bottom edges of the two triangles formed in (b). See diagram (d).

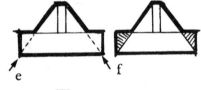

e. Turn the hat over, folded triangle side down, and place it flat on the table top. Fold the flap on that side up as in diagram (d). Fold both corners of the turned-up flap down between the body of the hat and the flap on the other side, as indicated by the dotted lines and arrows on diagram (e).

f. Fold the two remaining corners of the turned-up flap on the under side of the hat up and secure them with staples or tape (diagram (g)).

h. Turn to page 58 to find out how to make a paper plume out of newspaper. Tape plume by its top and bottom to the front of your hat.

2. **Sword**

a. Use four whole sheets of large newspaper (not tabloid size). Flatten all four sheets and stack them neatly, one on top of the next. Fold down corner (X) of all four stacked sheets so that it meets corner (Y) exactly, forming a perfect right-angled triangle. The shaded portion is the area outside the triangle. Cut away the shaded paper area with scissors, leaving a triangle. Open the triangle and flatten it on the table. You should have a perfect square of stacked newspaper.

b. Place the square of stacked newspaper sheets flat on the table, making sure that the center fold lies horizontal, as shown. Looked at this way the square is a diamond. Keep all four sheets of newspaper perfectly stacked. Now roll up the bottom corner of all four sheets at one time, using a pencil as the core. Keep the pencil parallel to the center fold indicated by the dotted line (X,N).

c. When the whole sheet is firmly rolled into a tube, as solid as you can make it, tape it securely and remove the pencil.

d. Bend over the top portion of the tube as shown in diagram (d) to form the sword handle. Be sure to allow sufficient room inside this loop of paper tubing so that the palm of your hand fits it as shown in diagram (f), plus an extra 2½ cm (1″) to allow the bottom of the sword handle to be taped to the blade.

f. Cover the sword and hilt with silver wrapping paper for extra realism. Now you are ready to play crusader, knight, or one of the three musketeers. Should your sword bend or wear out it's easy to make another. This sword is safe if used reasonably. Never actually touch another person's body with such a sword and especially do not poke it into anyone's face or eye.

– 61 –

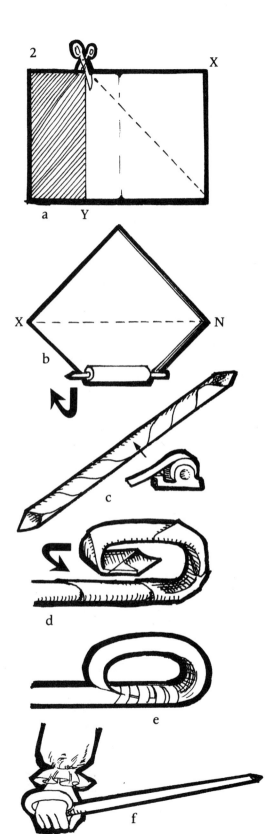

✂ Papier mâché

Making papier mâché costumes and parts has many advantages. They are lightweight. They can be decorated in many different colorful ways. They withstand frequent and repeated play and wear. Papier mâché costume-making takes time. It is especially important to allow ample drying time. Finished parts should not be placed in an oven to speed drying. They will shrink and warp.

It's best to work over an "armature." This consists of the desired shape constructed quite roughly and crudely out of plastic mesh, chicken or other wire, bits and pieces of corrugated and other board or paper, and materials, stapled or taped together. These shapes can be overlaid, refined and detailed with papier mâché and, when dry, painted with poster paints.

Making papier mâché. Cut newspaper or tissue paper into long strips, each roughly two and a half to three and a half cm (1″–1½″) wide. In a bowl or bucket make paste, mixing ordinary flour and water to the consistency of heavy cream. Add a few drops of oil of cloves, available at any drugstore. It prevents the paste from spoiling and keeps insects away. Wallpaper paste, rubber cement and acrylic medium, thinned to the same consistency, are equally useful, though more expensive. Soak the paper strips in the paste for about fifteen minutes and you are ready to work.

Working with papier mâché. Pick out one strip of paste-soaked paper at a time. Lay it on or wind it round the armature, being sure to cover edges as well, adding strip after strip, one laid next to and overlapping the other, in as many successive layers as needed to form the object or costume part. Three to five layers of paper strips are usually sufficient. More will add strength. Fine detail can be added with smaller strips, with wadded pieces of papier mâché, and with string, rope or other materials attached with papier mâché.

When the object is finished, set it on a shelf and allow it to dry completely. This may take several days, depending on the amount of papier mâché laid over the armature, on dampness and on the weather. Once thoroughly dry, the object can be sanded, cut with knife or jigsaw to form arm and neck holes, or drilled to add straps for wear. Other appendages made out of papier mâché, cardboard, plastic or foil can be adhered with paste or glue and, if necessary, further papier mâché strips added.

The thoroughly dry papier mâché object can be painted with poster colors and, if it is to be used or worn frequently or out of doors, waterproofed with several light coats of clear shellac. Be sure to let each coat of shellac dry before applying the next. Acrylics don't need waterproofing.

The following pages suggest basic working methods for costumes and accessories that can be made with papier mâché. Helmets, hats, suits of armor, leggings, jewelry, shields, swords and other props, funny clown noses, masks, outsize buttons and linked belts made out of papier mâché can be convincing, invite invention, and are lots of fun to make.

1

2

3

✄ Making large shapes out of papier mâché

The pictures on these two pages show how to make body armor. The same method can be used for making any other large shape out of papier mâché. Make a pattern out of newspaper or brown wrapping paper that fits your body contours. Then cut and bend corrugated cardboard to fit the pattern exactly. Add details roughed out with bundled newspaper, paper, box parts, tubes, plastic coffee can lids, and any other materials, attached to the basic armature with tape, string, or staples. Cover the roughly constructed armature with several layers of papier mâché strips, as described on pages 62-63.

Body armor

1. Make the pattern out of newspaper. Fit it to your body. Make wedge-shaped cuts into the paper until all portions are taped or stapled to fit closely to your body's contours without wrinkling. Flatten the paper pattern and trace it onto a sheet of corrugated cardboard cut from a supermarket carton. Bend cut portions to fit, and tape or staple them firmly in place. Make a matching piece for the back portion of the armor.

2. Fasten the cardboard armature together with brown paper or masking tape. Get someone to help you fit both halves — front and back — to your body. Protect your clothing with clear plastic.

3. Cut the two halves — front and back — apart.

4. Tape both halves firmly to separate sheets of cardboard or wrapping paper, after stuffing each with crumpled tissue or newspaper to support the weight of the papier mâché while it dries.

5. Cover both front and back armor with several layers of papier mâché strips. Let them dry completely. It may take a day or two.

6. Once both halves have dried, trim away excess paper, then further details, decorations, and coats of arms can be added with wadded paper, twine, small cut-out cardboard shapes. Cover these with extra layers of papier mâché. Paper, left to soak in paste for several days, turns into a mash that can be used like clay or putty.

For instructions on how to paint fully dried papier mâché sculptured costume parts, see page 113. Be sure to paint straps and other accessories at one and the same time so that matching parts are the same metallic or other color. Glue strips of felt or wadded cloth round the inside of arm holes and neckline to prevent rubbing.

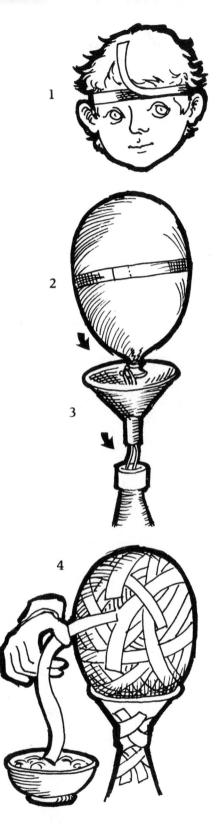

✂ Papier mâché hats and helmets

1. Measure your head's circumference, above the eyebrows, using tape, a strip of paper, or a ribbon.
2. Blow up a balloon until it fits the inside of the measuring tape headband. Then remove it and give the balloon an extra puff or two of air and tie it off. It should be about one and a quarter to two and a half cm (½"–1") larger than the measuring headband to allow for later shrinkage of the papier mâché.
3. Tie a heavy string around the knotted opening of the balloon. Pass this string through the neck of a funnel. Then tie a button or a burnt matchstick to the bottom of the string and wind and knot it so that the balloon is wedged firmly into the large opening of the funnel. Insert and tape the thin neck of the funnel into the neck of a heavy bottle. This will anchor the balloon so that you can work with it.
4. See pages 62-63 for details on how to make and work with papier mâché. Cover the balloon with papier mâché strips in sufficient layers until it forms a helmet shape strong enough to wear once it is dry and has been trimmed. This same basic shape can be used as the base for any number of different hats, animal heads and masks.

5. When the papier mâché has dried thoroughly and is no longer "springy" to the touch, remove funnel and bottle, deflate the balloon and pull it out of the bottom opening of the papier mâché headshape. Draw an oval opening for your face and enlarge the neck hole so that the helmet can be worn in comfort. At the start, cut all openings smaller than required. It's easier to cut and enlarge them, than to make them smaller by adding papier mâché.

6. An empty plastic yoghurt container makes a handsome crestholder into which feathers can be fitted later. Slit the top edge of the container into tabs all around; spread them and tape the container upside down to the top of the helmet. Adhere the tabs to the helmet with papier mâché strips.

7. and 8. Make a visor out of bent or scored cardboard. Drill holes with an awl through the sides of the helmet and attach the visor with paper clips from inside out so that it can be raised or lowered over the eyes. Cover sharp edges of paper clip with cardboard disk or cork (diagram 8).

See page 113 for directions on how to paint and preserve papier mâché.

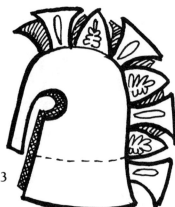

✂ **Papier mâché hats and helmets** (*continued*)

1. **Plumed helmet.** Finish the helmet by glueing paper or real feathers or plumes into a hole cut into the crest (see page 58).

2. **Viking helmet.** Make the basic shape of papier mâché (see pages 66, 67).

a. Cut a pie-shaped piece, as shown, out of heavy construction paper or light cardboard for each horn of the Viking's helmet. Cut tabs along the curved edge. Fold along the dotted line as shown.

b. Make curved cuts along the folded edge as shown. Be sure not to cut through the edge of the paper. Open out as in diagram (a).

c. Form the paper into a cone and tape the cone along its straight edge. Now gently curve the horn, keeping the cuts on the outer curve. Fold up tabs and glue each horn to the papier mâché, balloon-shaped helmet.

Form the headband and noseguard of the helmet out of corrugated cardboard. This, or any other helmet, can be decorated with wooden beads, game board playing counters, buttons and other accessories that can be glued to it and painted.

3. **Greek helmet.** Draw and cut portions from the formed helmet so that the final results looks like the profile shown here. Cut a cardboard collar to fit around the neck, below the chin. Staple it on and cover with papier mâché. Bend the noseguard outward and, if it cracks, add a couple of layers of papier mâché to stiffen it in its new position.

4. **Crest for Greek helmet.** Cut a rectangle of cardboard long enough to reach from crown to bottom edge at the back of the helmet. Use string to measure the distance (see diagram 3). Mark a double line down the center of the strip, as shown, and draw decorative scallops along both sides. Glue the center strip to the crest of the helmet. Fold up the scalloped sides after cutting them so that they remain hinged to the center strip. Glue the center strip to the helmet, letting the bent-up sides stand away from it. Cover with one or two layers of papier mâché strips.

5. **Horned medieval helmet.** Once the basic papier mâché base has dried, shape it as shown, to frame the face. Make two large horns out of thick construction paper, leaving tabs at the wide ends by which to glue them to the helmet (see (a) and (b)). Cover horns and helmet with papier mâché. While the last layer is still wet, inlay it with paper doilies. Let it dry thoroughly and finish (see page 113).

6. **Greaves** (see also pages 56-57). Make a pattern out of stiff paper, enclosing the whole lower leg. Fit the patterns carefully to both legs, cut two sets of matching shapes out of corrugated cardboard. Stuff each taped-together set with wadded newspaper and cover their outsides with layers of papier mâché. When dry, cut away a strip from the outside of each greave, wide enough to slip them on without cracking them. Punch two rows of holes along edges of each opening to allow you to lace them with thong or rope.

Decorate and paint as described on page 113.

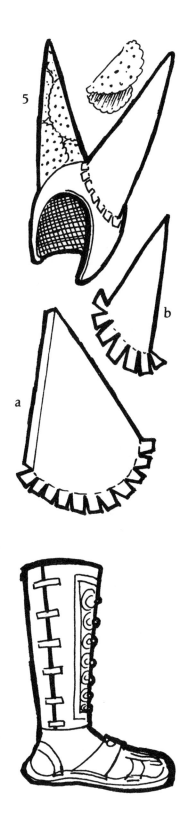

✂ Hats

You can tell who is who and who does what by the kind of hat he or she wears. It's easy to see how a different hat transforms the same face, shown above, into a king, a cook, or a politician. A nurse, fireman, or an admiral can be similarly recognized by their hats. A clown, jester, or dunce depends largely on his hat to make him look funny. Hats are essential parts of costuming. As much as keeping heads warm, hats were symbols of honor and respectability in the past. The members of different craft guilds in the Middle Ages recognized one another by hats alone.

It's not difficult to make a hat for your costume. The hat size must be carefully measured and fitted. Be sure to make a paper pattern of crown and rim before cutting the final material.

1. **Circumference** "W" the measurement round your head just above the eyebrows. Use a tape measure, ribbon or strip of paper long enough to fit round your head. Mark the ends of the strip exactly where they meet. This is your "W" measurement, shown on all the diagrams here and on following pages. Lay the marked strip out flat on the table. Add a centimeter (½″) or so at both ends as glue laps, or for stapling.

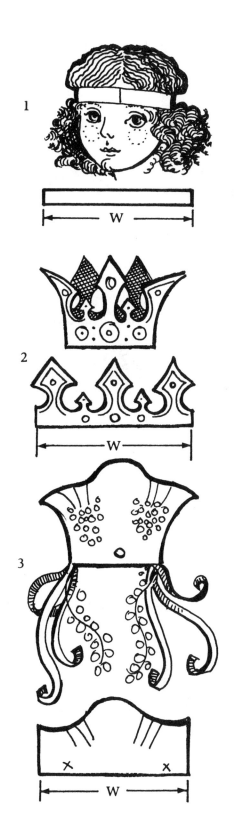

2. **Crown.** Cut the crown out of thin cardboard onto which the flattened "W" measurement has been traced. Don't forget the glue laps at both ends. Paint or decorate the crown while it is flat, using foil, glitter, twine, colored cardboard shapes, and silver or gold painted doilies as decorations. Then glue or staple the glue laps together. The crown should fit perfectly. If too large, you can make it smaller by pasting thin paper or cloth strips inside the edge of the rim.

3. **Ukrainian festival hat.** The same principle of making such hats hold true, whether it's to be a crown, an Indian's headdress, or, as in this illustration, a Ukrainian festival hat. Make the pattern as shown in diagram to fit the "W" measurement. Make cuts along the top edges, as shown, and bend the flanges outward. Decorate with sequins and ribbons.

Now make hats of your own invention . . . a Mad Hatter's hat, or a Mickey Mouse hat. Each can be made out of a single strip of heavy paper or lightweight cardboard fitted round your head, with other parts added, as required.

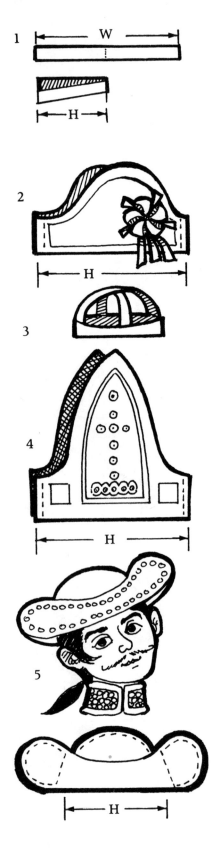

1. W
H

2. H

3.

4. H

5.

H

✂ **Hats** (*continued*)

1. The hats shown on these two pages are made differently from those described on the previous pages. Measure the "W" headband circumference as before (see pages 70-71), and fold each measured length of paper or ribbon in half. This half measure is marked "H" on all diagrams on these pages. For all hats shown here, cut two shapes, identical to those illustrated, each measuring "H" at the headband.

Allow about two and a half cm (1″) on both sides of the "H" width headband side on one of the two shapes cut out, to use as laps for glueing or stapling the two halves of the hat together.

2. **Admiral's or General's hat.** Cut two matching shapes as shown. Glue or staple them together. Cover both with black, shiny paper or felt. Make and attach a rosette of ribbon or paper with a crushed foil center.

3. **Liner.** If such a hat does not stay in place, cut an old, worn-out hat or cap into the shape shown here, and sew or glue it inside the hatband. Such a liner can also be made out of cardboard strips.

4. **Bishop's or Priest's hat.** A British or Hessian soldier's hat in the reign of King George III is similarly shaped. Give such a hat texture by glueing paper doilies, crushed leaves or crumbled macaroni to the outside of the hat before painting it.

5. **Bullfighter's hat.** Cover both shapes with fabric and paint them black. Decorate the outside of the hat with glitter and punched out foil disks. Look up pictures of Spanish bullfighters' costumes for details.

✂ **Cloth hats**

Cloth hats can be made in the same manner as

those described on the previous page. Use the "H" measurement shown above for each of the two matching shapes at the headband. Add one and a quarter cm (¾") to the outside of each cloth shape (indicated by dotted lines on diagrams) for seams. Sew the seams while the hat is turned inside out.

6. **Toboggan or elf hat.** Use any available fabric. When sewn and then turned right side out, it will have a finished, professional look. Sew or staple on the pom-pom made out of wool (see page 41).

7. **Robin Hood hat.** Use green felt, if available, or any other stiff green fabric. Lay out the two matching halves as shown, leaving a wide measure below the "H" measure indicated by the dotted line. This extra fabric, turned up after sewing, becomes the wide brim of the hat. Add a real or a paper feather (see page 58). A Tyrolean hat is made according to the same pattern, but with a narrower brim.

8. **Jester's hat.** Use felt or any other stiff fabric of a different color for each half. If no different colored fabrics are available, the hat can be painted in two colors with fabric paints. Sew along the dotted lines shown in the diagram. After turning the sewn hat inside out, bend over the two pointed ends. If they don't flop over properly they can be shaped with bent, plastic-covered wire or pipe cleaners sewn or pasted inside each. Sew a small bell or pom-pom to the tip of each bent-over point of the hat.

It's faster to sew these and similar hats by machine. But even if sewn by hand they can be made quickly. If hand-sewn it's best to stitch twice round each hem or seam.

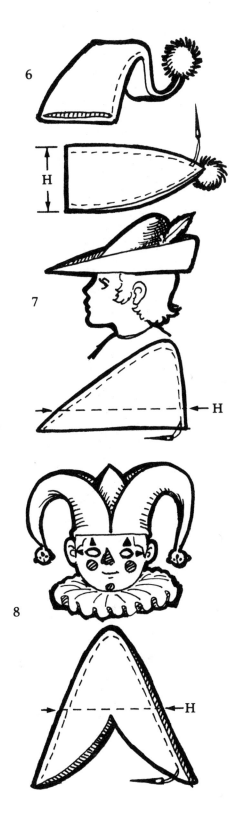

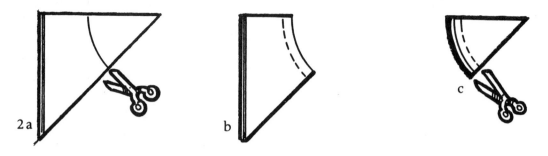

2a   b   c

Hat brims

Use the following method to fit wide-brimmed hats to your head. See pages 76-77 for fitting and attaching various hat crowns to such brims.

1. Fold a large square of wrapping paper or newspaper in half. Quarter it and then fold it into a triangle, along the dotted lines shown in diagram opposite.
2. Then, using a compass, draw a segment of a circle onto the triangle, inserting the point of the compass at the tip of the folded triangle. Cut along the drawn circle segment with scissors (see diagram 2(a)) and remove the tip of the triangle. When unfolded, the square of paper will show a hole cut into its center (see diagram 2).

1. **Fitting the brim.** Fit the unfolded paper square, with the hole cut out of its middle, on your head. Stand in front of a mirror. Don't force the paper on your head or it may tear. Gently pull the paper down and shape it until it begins to look like the brim of a floppy hat. If the hole is too small, remove the paper brim and enlarge the circle evenly all round (see diagram 2(b)). Be careful to cut away very little at a time. If enlarged by too much, you may have to add a circle of paper (see diagram 2(c)), taping it to the opening as shown in diagram.
2. The brim should fit loosely on your head, resting on the tips of your ears. The thickness of the felt or cloth used to make the brim finally will make it fit more closely.

Once the brim fits, remove it and flatten it on a table. It can then be used to design different hat brims shown in diagrams 3 to 8 on the opposite page.

3. **Witch's hat brim**   5. **Top hat or beaver hat brim**

4. **Fireman's brim**   6. **Three-cornered hat brim**

7. and 8. **Funny hat brims** for which no crown is needed. Just wear the rims (see 8b).

See pages 76-77 for instructions on how to make different hat crowns that fit these rims. You'll need two identical rims for each, fitting one over and the other below the tabs of the crowns, and pasting them to these tabs.

1

2

3

4

5

6

7

8

8b

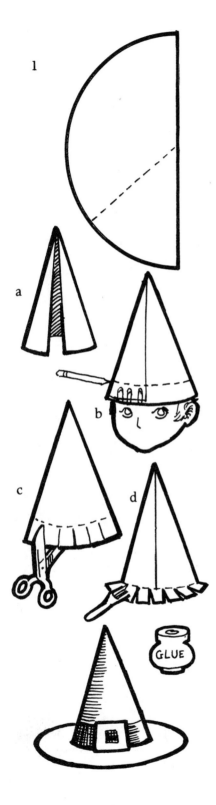

✂ Hat crowns

The hat crowns shown here can be fitted to different brims, for which construction methods are described and illustrated on pages 74-75. The hat crown, like the brim, must be fitted to your head before both are pasted together.

1. **Witch's hat crown.** Draw and cut a large semicircle out of newspaper or brown wrapping paper. See page 110 for instructions on how to draw a large circle with a string-and-pencil compass. Cut away the smaller pie-shaped piece at the dotted line. Form the cone shown in diagram (a), fasten the edges with paper clips, and fit it to your head as illustrated in (b). If too large, and if it slips down too far over your eyes, simply roll the cone up more tightly. Mark a line evenly all round the cone, just above the level of your eyes.

Make scissor cuts along the rim, up to the dotted line above eye level, as shown in diagram (c), to form tabs by which the crown can be pasted to the rim. Bend these tabs up, as shown in diagram (d).

Place the completed cone hat onto another sheet of thin, black cardboard and trace the pattern, including the tabs, on the black cardboard, using the point of a compass or a white colored pencil. Remove the paper pattern and cut the crown of the hat out of cardboard.

Form and glue the cardboard cone as detailed above. Leave the paper clips in place until the glue has dried completely. Cut, and bend up tabs. Prepare two brims for a witch's hat (see diagram 3, page 75). Spread glue on top of tabs only. Slide one hat brim down over the cone and press its underside to the glue-covered tabs. Then glue the second brim to the underside of the first to make it stiffer and to cover up the glue tabs. Hold in place with paper clips until dry, as before.

Add hat band and buckle, made of cardboard-covered foil. An elastic band, fitted under the chin and attached on opposite sides to the rim where it joins the cone hat, will hold the witch's hat firmly in place.

2. and 3. Pilgrim father's hat or fez (see page 76, 1). Diagram 3 shows the shape of the sides of the crown. The line above the tabs, cut into the bottom edge, is that at which this hat should rest on your brow. The dotted line on one long edge shows the glue lap at which it is fastened to the opposite one. Diagram 2 shows the top of the hat. The line at which the glue laps are attached should match the smaller, top opening of the crown. Bend down the glue laps and paste them inside the top of the crown. Use the same brim for pilgrim father's hat as that used for the witch's hat. The fez needs no brim.

4. Fireman's hat crown. Paste the sides to the center, using the glue laps as shown. The tabs on the far left of the diagram are pasted to the inside of the far right edge. Paste all glue laps UNDER the sides. The matching hat brim (diagram 4) and instructions for making it, are described on pages 74-75. (a) shows side view of assembled hat, (b) is the back view.

5. Cossack fur hat or Busby, top hat, or Beaver hat. Fur hats don't need brims. Cut and assemble in the same manner as that required for the pilgram father's hat described in 2 and 3 above, except that the wide and narrow portions are reversed. Attach the top as in 2. See pages 74-75 for making the required brims. Attach them, as described above and as shown in diagram 6, passing the crown's tabs through the brim opening, pasting them to the brim from below. Then paste the second brim to the first, hiding the glue tabs.

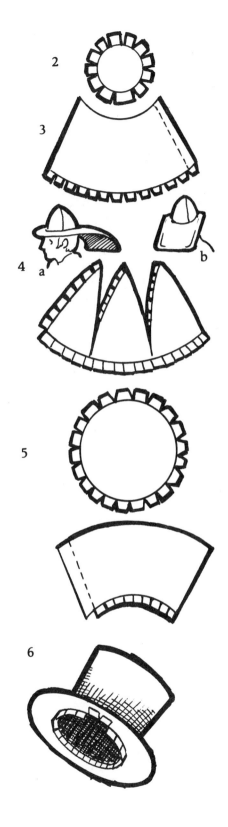

✂ Gathered cloth hats

Gathered cloth hats as shown here can be made out of a large circle of fabric (see diagram 2). Turn to page 110 to find out how to make a large circle without compasses. The edge of the circle can be hemmed, finished with lace or binding, or kept from unraveling by covering it with a thin film of glue or nail polish.

1. **Mob cap.** After making the cloth disk described above, thread a needle with strong thread and gather the fabric all round the edge of the circle, two, three, or more cm (¾″, 1¼″) from the edge. When the thread has been sewn all round the cloth disk, pull up on the ends until the opening thus formed fits your head. The more space you leave between the edge of the cloth circle and the gathering stitches, the longer the ruffles will be that frame your face.

3 and 4. **Granny hat.** Cut a large cloth or crepe paper disk and leave a very wide strip between its edge and the circle at which you gather it.

5. **Chef's hat.** Cut the same cloth disk as described in 1. Cut a stovepipe crown (see diagram (a) and pages 70-71) to fit your "W" measurement. This crown can be made out of starched fabric or fabric-covered cardboard. Glue, staple, or sew the gathered cloth disk to the top opening of the stovepipe crown. Paint the whole hat white, unless white cloth and cardboard are used.

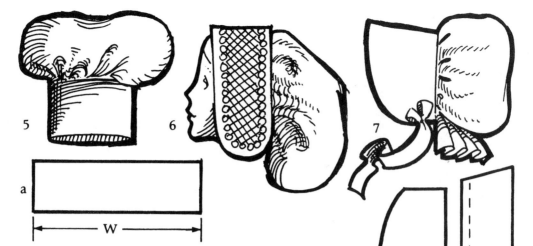

5

6

a

|← W →|

6. **Lady Jane hat.** Make a frame that fits round your head and cheeks out of quilted fabric or cloth-covered cardboard. Bend it gently to fit your face. Glue, staple or sew a gathered cloth disk to it, round the top, leaving the bottom of gathered disk free, as shown. Decorate this hat with sequins, sewn-on imitation pearls or foil disks. Use a piece of elastic under your chin to hold it on, or pin it on with bobbypins.

7. **Poke bonnet.** This is so named because a "poke" (paper bag) was sewn into the brim (diagram a) to make it stiff. You can make poke brim patterns out of cloth-covered stiff paper or lightweight cardboard and fit them to your face, before attaching a gathered cloth disk as described in 1. Add ties and a "sun ruffle" (diagram b) sewn below the place where the poke brim and the gathered crown join.

8. **Railroader's cap.** The gathered cloth disk fits on the back of the headband. The visor (a) is attached to the front of the headband, as shown by diagrams (a) and (b). Make the headband (b) fit your "W" measurement (see page 71). It should be made out of sturdy starched cloth, felt or cardboard. Attach the visor to the headband at the glue tabs. Sew or staple the gathered cloth disk to the rear of the headband.

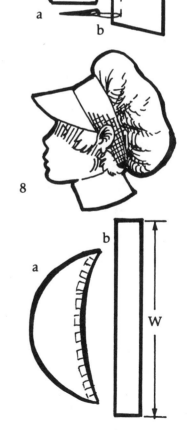

7

a   b

8

a   b

W

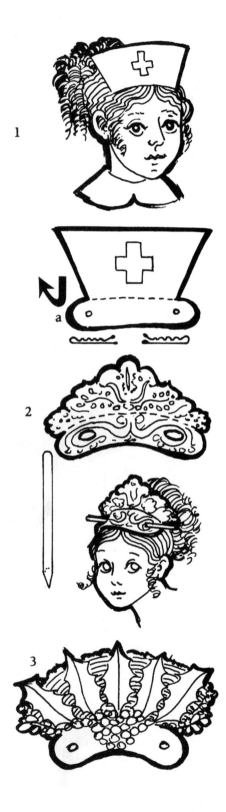

✄ Paper hats

1. **Nurse's or Waitress's cap.** Any hats that stands up, like those shown here, can be made quickly out of stiff paper. Design the stand-up portion flat and then add the longer, narrow strip at the bottom, as shown in diagram (a). Paste both together and then transfer the whole design to construction paper or other lightweight cardboard. Use a ballpoint pen to engrave a deep groove into the line at which the narrow strip joins the larger shape. Be sure not to cut through the material. This is called a "score." Punch a hole at each end of the narrow strip and then bend it back, along the score. Pin this cap to your head with two bobbypins, each passed through the holes punched into the strip.

2. **Ballerina headdress or tiara.** Use the same method as described in 1, except that the scored strip is bent forward. It can be attached to the hair with bobbypins as before, with a chopstick or with a plastic knitting needle passed through the holes and your hair, as shown. Alternately, an elastic band can be attached to the holes and passed back under your hair at the back of the head. Such a tiara can be made out of taffeta, stiffened with iron-on stiffener, and decorated with fake, sew-on jewels.

3. **Christmas or seasonal hair ornament.** This can be made along the same lines as those described in 1 and 2 above, and decorated with seasonal ornaments or foliage.

4. **Cut-out paper hat.** This hat is made with traditional "Polish" paper cuts. Fold a square sheet of paper along the dotted lines shown. Then draw a segment of a circle onto the folded shape, inserting the point of the compass into the pointed tip (see diagram (a)). Cut along this circle with a pair of scissors. Then make scissor cuts alternately on each side, without cutting all the way through. Each such cut should come to within about 5 mm (1/8″) of the edge (see diagram (b)).

Then unfold the shape and flatten it. Pull gently up at the center to form the hat shown in diagram (c). Such a hat can be especially attractive if two different colored squares of paper are pasted together before folding and cutting them. The finished hat can also be decorated with paper or real leaves, flowers, ribbon and other ornaments, inserted between the cut and extended paper.

Experiment with this technique. Leave wider or narrower brims turned up or down, front or back. This same paper cutting technique can be used to make decorative flower baskets. Simply turn the cut and extended paper shape upside down and attach a paper handle. Try out identical cuts on differently shaped and folded pieces of paper or foil to make a variety of costume ornaments or jewelry.

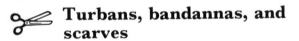

✂ Turbans, bandannas, and scarves

A variety of head coverings can be made by twisting and tying a length of cloth. Such hats are worn in many parts of the world.

1. **Arabian turban.** Make a fez, as described on page 77. Then use an ordinary silk scarf or a patterned square of other light cloth to make the turban. Twist the scarf into a long spiral as shown in diagram (a) before draping it round the fez. Experiment with different twisted, draped effects. Then secure the ends of the twisted fabric with a shiny brooch or pin. Hang a string of fake pearls or beads round the fez and down over the front of the turban as shown in illustration (b). Both Babushka (2) and Pirate scarf (3) are draped with third point down — see diagram (2a).

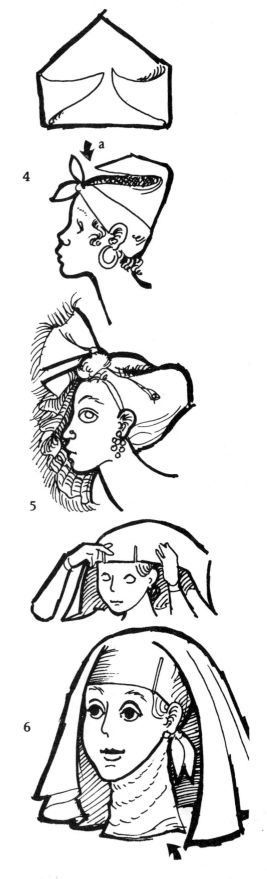

2. **Babushka or peasant scarf.** Use a large square of decorative fabric or a scarf. Fold it diagonally and bend down the corners as shown. Pull the folded edge of the scarf against your forehead and tie the narrow, pointed ends at the back of your head and under the hair letting the third point hang loose.

3. **Pirate scarf.** Fold a square of cloth or a scarf as in 2(a). Pull the small, pointed ends of the cloth round your head and tie them at the back or on one side of the head over the third, doubled corner. Let the narrow, knotted ends hang down, but tuck the doubled corner up under the headband to form a tight-fitting cap.

4. **African turban.** Fold a square of cloth or a scarf as in 2(a). Place the folded edge of the cloth against the nape of the neck at the back of your head. Pull up on the pointed ends and tie them in front, just above the forehead. Pull the loose, wide corners of the cloth up over the back of the head, as shown in illustration 4(a), and tuck them under the knot in front, thus covering the whole head.

5. **Indonesian head scarf.** Use a rectangle of material with raveled or fringed edges at the shorter ends. Wrap the back of the head in the cloth and tie the gathered ends into a knot just above the forehead.

6. **Nun or Madonna head covering.** Pull a scarf or any other large piece of square or rectangular fabric across your forehead. Pin the cloth at either temple with a bobbypin. Tie or pin the bottom corners of the fabric behind your head and then bring the fullness of the rest of the cloth forward to hide the pins.

– 83 –

✂ Pipe cleaner headdresses

1. **Egyptian headdress.** This and many kinds of African headdresses can be made with a handful of pipe cleaners, black wool, and a package of drinking straws or macaroni.

a. The cobra ornament, shown in full front view, is worn at the forehead and can be cut out of cardboard and then painted. Fold the cut-out cobra head along the dotted line and shape it gently with your fingers before attaching it to the headband.

b. Twist pipe cleaners together to form a large circle that fits round your head. Then add spokes, made out of additional pipe cleaners twisted together to lengths somewhat greater than the diameter of the circle. When fitted over your head, the circle with the spokes attached should form the close-fitting cap shown in diagram (c). Cut straws or macaroni into short lengths. Disassemble the pipe cleaner cap and string the straw or macaroni sections on the wires, being sure to leave sufficient uncovered wire at the ends to allow them to be twisted and reassembled as before.

c. Attach the cardboard cobra shown in diagram 1(a) to the front of the head covering. It can be glued on or fastened with additional pipe cleaner wire.

d. String beads, straw or macaroni sections onto black thread, wool, or pipe cleaners, to form strands long enough to reach from the circular rim of the headdress to your shoulders. The designs shown here are samples of some of the possible combinations. Tie or twist one strand next to the other, in between the beaded sections of the circle that forms the base of the head covering shown in illustrations 1 and 1(b).

2   3

Braids of black wool hung between each pendant bead, straw, or macaroni section-covered strand will help fill out the headdress. Straws are lightest, but a bead or macaroni section is more likely to keep its shape. Your own hair should also be worn braided and tied with black thread under the head covering (see pages 96-97).

2. and 3. **Pipe cleaner wreaths.** Twist a sufficient number of pipe cleaners end to end to form a circle that reaches round your head. Staple or paste stems of real or paper flowers and leaves to the circle of pipe cleaners to form any variation of the wreaths shown.

"Found" hats

4. **Cavalier's hat.** Turn up one side of the brim of one of mother's discarded, wide-brimmed sun hats. Pin the turned-up side and decorate it with a large paper cut plume (see page 58).

5., 6., 7., 8., and 9. All these are "found" objects that can be worn as costume hats exactly as they are. Can you discover other things in your home that are suitable to wear as hats?

4

5

6

7

8

9

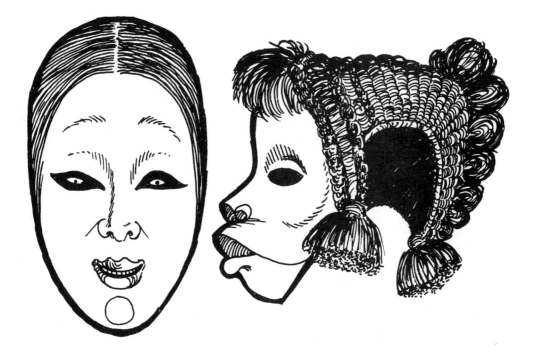

✂ Masks

A mask creates a barrier of make-believe between yourself and the rest of the world. You can hide behind it. No one will know who you are. You simply disappear, since most people recognize you only by your face. This is the reason why many people throughout the world believe that there is magic in wearing a mask. By putting one on you actually become whatever it represents — another person, animal or spirit. While wearing it you can achieve things you could not ordinarily do.

Masks, therefore, like the spirits or characters they represent, reflect the feelings, impulses, wishes and fears of those who create and wear them. Some masks are intended to give warriors courage. Others are designed to represent or drive out evil spirits. Some poke fun or make their wearers more beautiful or terrifying.

Masks are still worn by many tribes for healing, and for ritual dances at marriages, births, funerals and during initiation rites. Those shown here come from many different parts of the world. Don't copy them. They are intended as inspirations for you to make your own kind of mask. Use an ordinary sheet of paper, with holes cut into it for eyes and mouth. More elaborate masks can be made with papier mâché, as described on the following pages, complete with hair, detailed, pasted-on features, and painted-on make-up.

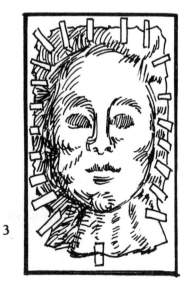

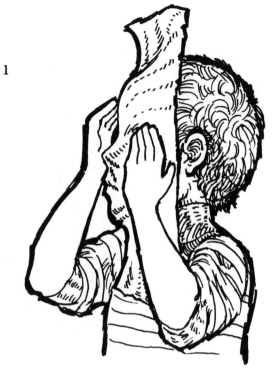

✂ Papier mâché masks

1. **Making a life mask.** Take a large sheet of heavy-duty aluminum foil. Stand in front of a mirror and press the foil against your face, covering every part. Using the tip of one finger, poke small holes into the foil at your nostrils, to allow you to breathe. When you have patted the foil to fit the contours of your face, remove it gently. Use a pair of sharp scissors to cut out the eyes. Then try on the foil mask once more. You'll be able to see whether it fits and shows all your features (see illustration (a)).

2. and 3. When you are satisfied that the foil mask fits you perfectly, remove it gently once more. Hold it, face down, in the palm of one hand and fill the hollow mask with crushed and wadded tissue paper, and place a piece of cardboard on top. Then turn the tissue-filled foil mask right side up. Tape it to the sheet of heavy cardboard. It should be larger all round than the mask itself, as shown in 3.

4. Turn to pages 62-63 for instructions on how to mix and form with papier mâché. Cover the foil mask with at least three layers of overlapping papier mâché strips. Be sure to follow all details without pressing the foil mask out of shape, Let the papier mâché dry thoroughly. This may take a day or two.

   When the papier mâché has dried completely, remove it from the foil mold. Trim away all rough edges and cut nostrils, eyes and, if you wish, a mouth opening out of the papier mâché mask. Try it on. It should fit you almost exactly.

5. Now add a funny nose, heavy eyebrows, fat cheeks, horns, outsize ears, or any other special feature to your mask to give it character. These and other attachments can be made out of cardboard, paper, or papier mâché, glued or pasted to the mask. When all added details are in place, cover the whole mask with one or two additional layers of papier mâché strips. Be careful not to moisten the mask too much or it may warp out of shape.

6. When fully dry, sand, paint, add hair and other details. Then wear the mask and delight or scare your friends. You'll discover how frightening you look to others when you go about in disguise. Hang your mask on the wall in your room when you aren't wearing it.

Attach the mask to your face by a length of elastic or ribbon, fastened to small holes, pierced close to the edge on each side of the mask.

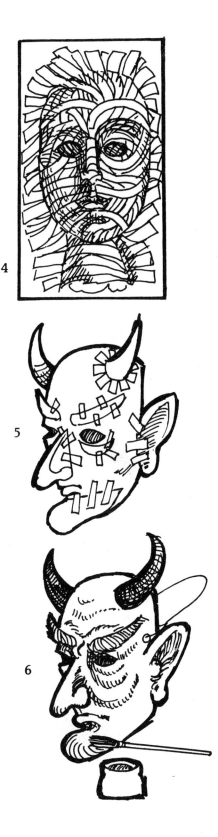

4

5

6

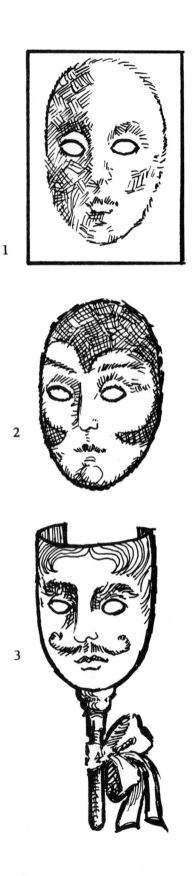

✂ **Masks** *(continued)*

1. and 2. A cheesecloth or linen mask can be formed over an aluminum foil mold in a manner identical to the method described on pages 88-89. Form the foil mold as before, stuff it with crumpled tissue paper and tape it to a sheet of heavy cardboard. Then choose or dye a length of linen or cheesecloth in the desired color, using vegetable dyes. Soak the dyed fabric in a highly concentrated solution of starch. While still moist, form the cloth over the foil mold. Let it dry on the mold. Lift it off the foil gently and trim away excess edges. Paint and decorate it, and attach a ribbon or elastic band by which to wear it.

   When made of cheesecloth, such a mask can be especially eerie since your skin color will show through. Be sure to keep the mask on the foil mold between times of use, so that it retains its shape.

3. Any mask can be glued to a wooden handle decorated with ribbon or lace. It is then held before your face, and it can be hung from the waist when not in use.

4. A pair of old eyeglass frames to which false eyebrows are pasted, and a funny nose to which a mustache is glued make an effective disguise. No one will recognize

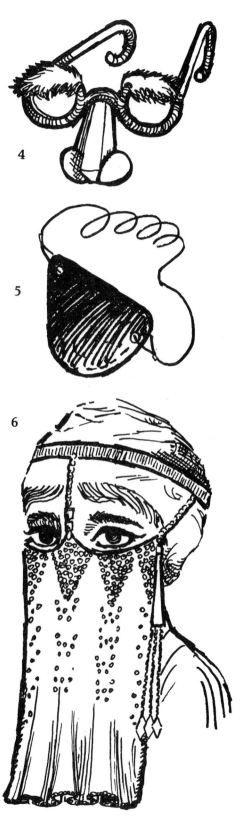

you, even though only a part of your face is covered.

5. You can buy an eyepatch at any drugstore for a few pennies. It will turn you into a pirate or Moshe Dayan. Or you can make your own eyepatch out of stiffener, black fabric, and a length of elastic.

6. Veils like those worn by ladies and by female slaves in the *Arabian Nights* can be quickly improvised with sheer, flowing material cut from a discarded slip, a silk scarf, drapery fabric sample, or an old dress. An elastic band, hook-and-eye fasteners, and paper or other costume jewelry will make you look mysterious and oriental.

7. A half mask worn only over the eyes and the bridge of the nose is yet another convincing disguise. Such masks were popular throughout Europe in the 17th and 18th centuries. Make a foil mold, as described on pages 88-89. Stuff it with crushed tissue paper and attach, right side up, to thick cardboard, as before. Then form a half mask with papier mâché or with starched fabric. Trim and decorate it when dry, and attach to your head with elastic. Such a half mask is useful for wear with an animal costume when you choose not make a full head mask.

✂ Make-up

If you live in a city and have money to spend, you can find a theatrical costumer or supply house where professional stage make-up, putty for false noses, grease paint and other accessories can be bought. Be sure to read package and jar labels and follow the instructions for applying and removing make-up. Some cosmetics can cause skin rashes. Others require a special base for application or solvents to remove them.

You can have fun and disguise yourself effectively even with ordinary household materials and with things that can be found on mother's dressing table, if she'll allow it.

For the chalky-white look appropriate for a clown, a doll or a ghost, cover your face and neck with zinc oxide ointment or vaseline first. Then powder it with several applications of talcum powder or corn flour. Be sure to hold your breath while powdering your face.

Use your mother's eyebrow pencil, or a burnt cork, to draw heavy eyebrows, a mustache, goatee, sideburns, freckles, dark "worry" lines, or stipple our cheeks to give yourself a dark, unshaven hobo look. Your mother's or older sister's lipstick, rouge and mascara or eye shadow are sufficient for most other make-up needs. Either may be willing to share their make-up accessories with you, if you'll use just a little.

1. **Scull cap or wig base**

a. Pull a cut-off white stocking or section of white panty hose over your hair. Mark a line on the stocking all around your forehead, below and around sideburns and around your ears, using a make-up grease pencil or felt marker. Have someone else mark the nape of your neck on the stocking.

b. Push the dangling toe portion of the stocking inside the cap and ask someone to mark the place on top or at the back where the tuck is made. Remove the cap carefully and sew the tucked-in portion securely with thread that matches the color of the stocking.

c. Cut away the extra fabric at the marked line. The cap can be held in place with white adhesive tape, skin colored bandaids or surgical tape just below the sideburns and at the nape of the neck. Or elastic can be sewn to each sideburn of the cap and held in place under your chin. Be sure that the elastic is loose and does not fit tightly or else it may cut off circulation or be uncomfortable.

2. **Clown noses**

a. If nose putty is unavailable, you can make funny noses out of papier mâché, a ping-pong ball, or a section cut out of a thick sheet of styrofoam packaging material. Wedge the shape into an open dresser drawer. Then, using pointed scissors, cut out a hole that fits your nose (see diagram (a)). Try it on and make sure that your nostrils remain uncovered. Cover any sharp edges with surgical tape (see diagram (b)).

b. Paint the ping-pong ball or styrofoam shape with bright red paint. Don't use nail polish; it may dissolve the plastic material. Adhere to face with surgical tape or adhesive.

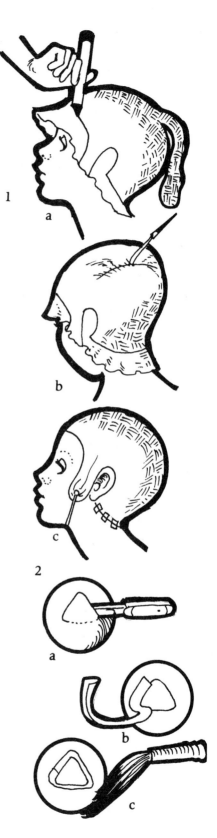

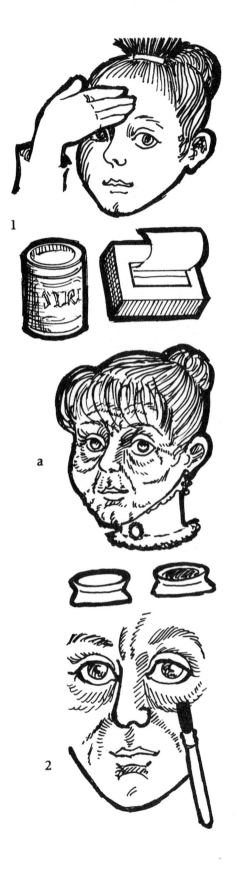

1. **Looking old and wrinkled.** Mix equal parts of water and clear sugar syrup in a bowl. Apply this mixture evenly all over your face and neck. Then, before the mixture has dried on your skin, cover all portions of your face, except eyes, nostrils and mouth, with sheets of pink, yellow, or peach-colored facial or toilet tissue. Don't smile or talk while the sugar-and-water-adhered tissue dries on your face. Once it has dried, wrinkle and crinkle your skin and forehead; make faces; and open your mouth as wide as you can. The adhered tissue paper will wrinkle, bulge and crease so that you won't recognize yourself.

a. To enhance the ageing, use eye shadow to paint dark circles under your eyes and sharp lines and wrinkles at the corners of your mouth and eyes. Follow the contours and direction of the lines in the crinkled tissue paper adhered to your skin. After the party or play the whole mess will wash off your face easily with warm water and soap. Be sure not to flush the tissues down the toilet as they will clog it.

2. **How to look really horrible.** If you should choose to turn yourself into a witch, monster, or lizard, paint your face as before, using diluted, clear sugar syrup. Then use blue, purple, white or green tissue paper and adhere it to your skin as described in 1. above. You can also glue feathers, rice, cottonseed or millet seeds to your sticky face to become totally repulsive. No one will recognize — or want to know — you.

3. **Mustaches.** Cut a length of wide surgical tape into the shape of the desired mustache. Look at yourself in the mirror, and tape the mustache gently to your image. You'll then be

able to tell just how you'll look, or make necessary changes in shape without pasting it to your face. Then make "hair" using frayed nylon stockings or cut-up yarn or wool. Cover the surgical tape mustache with acrylic medium paste while it still sticks to the mirror and adhere as much hair as required. Let the glue dry before removing the finished mustache from the mirror. Then wear it, patting the sticky side of the adhesive tape to your upper lip.

Unless you own and use real theatrical make-up, eyelash adhesive, or the surgical tape method described above, it's not a good idea to adhere fake hair, or fabric mustaches directly to your skin. Those described here can be removed with warm water and soap. Other adhesives may require strong solvents or alcohol that can be extremely dangerous when used near the eyes.

The same surgical tape technique, or eyelash adhesive, can be used for attaching sequins, jewels or beauty spots to your skin.

4. **Cat's whiskers** or any other animal hair can be drawn directly onto your skin with an eyebrow pencil, liquid eye-liner, or a burnt cork. They can be removed with warm water and soap or with cold cream.

5. **Beauty spots or mouches.** Ask your mother whether she has any "mouches." They are small, gummed, heart-, crescent- or other shaped pieces of velvet. They can be adhered to and removed from your skin without difficulty. The fashion dates back to the 17th century when ladies and gentlemen often wore several on their faces at one and the same time. You can also use gummed paper stickers which come in many sizes and shapes.

✂️ Braids and pigtails

The way you wear your hair is an essential part of costuming. Braids and plaits are among the most distinctive hair styles worn by men and women at various times in history all over the world. The very manner of braiding the hair has served to distinguish kings from commoners. How you braid your hair determines who you are. The number of braids and how they are wound around your head can determine your station and whom you represent.

Mexican and Indian girls braid bright ribbons and yarn into their hair. Braids can be curled round your ears, pulled across the top of or behind your head, made into loops or snails, or pinned into a variety of shapes. In Africa hair is braided into complex and beautiful patterns by different tribes. It would be impossible to show or describe all of them here. Look at books and photographs of people, customs and costumes from different countries. Most show indigenous hair styles.

Use netting, a stocking or paper forms (see page 80, diagram 1) as a base to which to pin, knot, glue or sew braids made of yarn. If you choose yarn that matches your hair color you can braid both together and achieve a full, braided look similar to that of the Roman lady shown in illustration 3. Egyptian braids should be numerous, close and full. Use yarn that matches your hair color and interbraid both. You can pin additional braids of yarn to your own hair to fill out the hairdo. See page 84 for other suggestions on how to make an Egyptian headdress.

Dampen your hair and then braid it into many tiny, closely braided strands (diagram 7) in order to achieve an extremely curly or wavy effect required for a gypsy or Lady Godiva disguise. Curl up the end of each little braid with a curler, string, or pipe cleaner. Let your hair remain in braids until it has dried completely. Then unwind the string or pipe cleaners; undo the braids carefully; and shake out your hair. It will be tightly curled and will stay that way, at least until the end of the performance or costume party. If you desire a wavy effect (see diagram 8), comb it out with your fingers after curling it as described above. If you want a truly frizzy effect, use a hair brush (9).

1

2

3

4

5

6

7

8

9

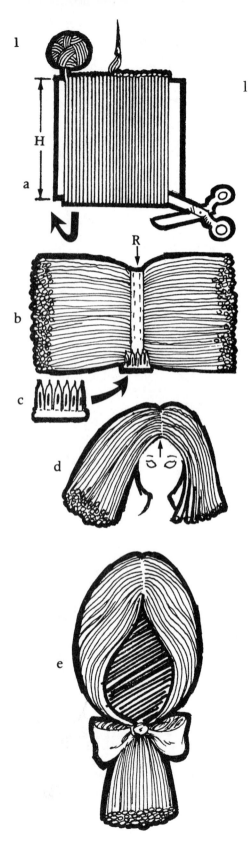

✂ Wigs

1. a. Find a large piece of heavy cardboard and cut it about 30 cm (12″) long, and 33 cm (13¼″) wide (see measure (H). Use a large ball of yarn to make the hair for the wig. Tape the end of the yarn to the bottom right hand corner of the cardboard. Then wind the yarn round and round the cardboard closely and continuously as shown in diagram (a). Cover the cardboard with about three layers of yarn. When you reach the end of the ball of yarn knot a new piece to its end and continue to wind. When the cardboard is fully covered, thread a large needle with strong thread of approximately the same color as the yarn. Tie the end of the thread to the last loop of yarn at the top right hand corner of the board. Use any simple stitch with which you are familiar to sew the yarn strands together along the top edge only. It's advisable to sew the yarn strands from one end of the cardboard to the other and back again to your starting point to hold them together firmly. This seam will be the "parting" in the hair of your wig. Then use the scissors to cut the yarn loose along the bottom edge of the cardboard, as shown.

    b. Remove the yarn from the board and place it flat on the table top, sewn side down. Reinforce the reverse of the sewn "part" by sewing drapery tape or ribbon (R) all along on the reverse side. If your mother owns a sewing machine, she can stitch such a tape onto the underside of the part for you. Suggest that she place a sheet of typing or bond paper under the wig while she sews, so that the loose yarn strands don't clog the machine. The paper will pull away easily after the reinforcement tape has been stitched to the wig.

    c. Sew a small comb into the front of the wig, teeth facing the back of the head as shown in diagram (b).

    d. Fasten the comb firmly at the center of your forehead by pushing the comb into your hair.

e. Trim and style the wig, using rubber bands, ribbon and other accessories appropriate to the period of your costume. To achieve the 19th-century-effect shown in the illustration, pull the wig hair down behind your head and fasten it with a rubber band at the nape of your neck. Cover the rubber band with a velvet or silk bow.

2. You need a stocking base (see page 93) as a head covering for other types of wigs you can make yourself. Pull hair, yarn, or silk embroidery thread through the mesh of the stocking cap with a crochet hook (2a). Then find an adjacent mesh opening and pull the rest of the thread through, forming a loop. Tie a knot in the loop and the "hair" will stay in place. The more and the closer such hairs are tied next to one another or to a stocking-cap, the fuller and more effective the wig will be when finished.

For a partially bald or shaven head wig, as for the Japanese hairdo shown in illustration 2(b), leave a portion of the stocking wig free of hair. Make sure that the color of the stocking wig matches the skin color or make-up of the character you portray. Choose a white stocking for the Japanese wig, shown here, since Japanese actors usually use white make-up for all exposed skin.

3. Use silk thread, if available, for this Japanese lady's wig, unless your own hair is long enough to be formed into the required traditional hairdo.

Sometimes second-hand wigs, discarded hair pieces, or old fur can be had inexpensively in second-hand and junk shops. Be sure to ask your mother to disinfect and wash them thoroughly before use. Synthetic fur, upholstery and rug remnants and samples can also often be bought for very little. They can be useful for turning you into an Abominable Snowman, elf, or wild animal.

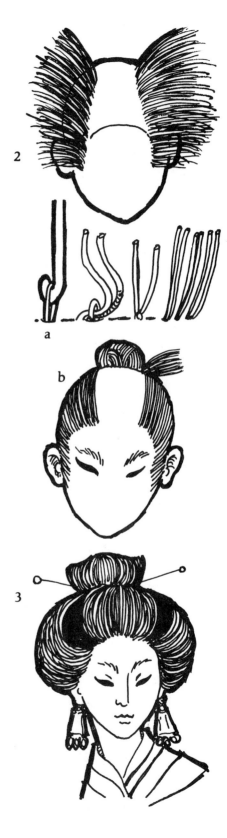

– 99 –

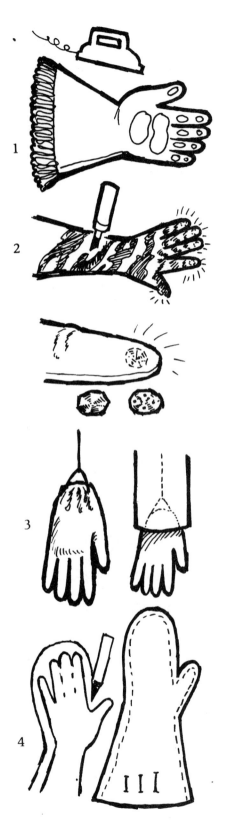

✂ Paws

1. Dye a pair of old gloves or mittens to match the rest of your costume (see pages 124-125). Use iron-on patches of a contrasting color to simulate the soft skin pads of animal feet.

2. **Cat or Tiger paws.** Use a laundry marker to stripe old gloves or mittens to make paws for a tiger or a cat. Continue the same stripe pattern up the sleeve of whatever discarded shirt you wear as part of your wild animal disguise. Costume jewelry, sequins, or foil pasted to the end of each finger will look like sharp claws, especially from a distance.

3. **False hands.** If you need your real hands for magic or stage business under your costume, if you choose to be Frankenstein's monster or a very tall person or a headless ghost, you may need a second, false pair. Stuff a pair of gloves with tissue paper until they are filled. Tie the wrist end of each glove with string and pin each to the inside of an empty costume sleeve.

4. **Mittens.** You can make your own mittens for a mailed armor fist or animal paw by first designing a pattern to fit your hand on newspaper or wrapping paper. Draw a full outline of your hand with magic marker. Add 1½ cm (½″) all around for the seams. Transfer the design to cloth, felt, or fake fur — two matching shapes for each hand. Cut out the cloth shapes and sew each set of two, inside out, along the seam indicated by the dotted line on the diagram. Sew buttons to the ends of your costume sleeves and make matching buttonholes on your mittens. They can then be buttoned on, giving your costume arm a fully covered continuous animal skin or armored appearance.

✂ Boots

Add fancy paper, felt or cloth cuffs to your rubber boots to turn them into soldier, guardsman, knight, Santa Claus, peasant or folk costume boots. Look at reference books and discover appropriate footwear decorations. Then cut the required cuff pattern out of paper: two halves for each boot cuff pattern (see diagram (a)). Fit them to the top opening of the boot, turning the upper edges into the boot.

Allow for seams when transferring the design to cloth or felt. Add sufficient fabric for overlap and tucking the cuffs into the boots. Then cut and sew each set of two together and decorate. Use lace cut-offs, doilies, ruffles, binding or laundry marker (see diagrams (c) and (d)). Let the boot cuff decorations match and be in keeping with the rest of your costume. Once decorated, the cuffs can be pasted or stapled into the rubber boot tops. You may wish to add buckles to the boots (see pages 102-103).

a

c

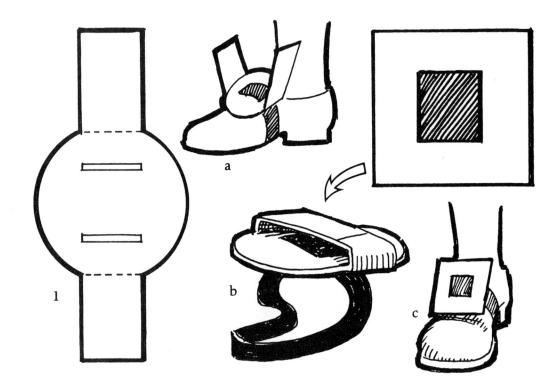

a

b

c

1

✂ Shoe buckles

Any large, shiny buckle attached to the top of a shoe changes its character and appearance and makes it a part of your costume. The buckles shown here are easily made and attached to ordinary footwear. They attach and slip off any shoe, leaving it undamaged for daily wear.

1. Use compasses and a ruler to draw the circle, slots and tabs shown. The rectangular tabs extending from the circle should be long enough so that, when bent together, they overlap and can be stapled or glued (see diagrams (a, b)). Make the two slots wide enough to allow you to thread elastic ribbon through both. You'll need two such cut-out shapes, one for each shoe. Measure and cut two pieces of elastic ribbon so that, when stretched and under some tension, each fits under your shoe's instep, and up and around the top of your shoe, with sufficient material left over so that the ends can be taped, glued, or stapled together (see diagrams (a), (b) and (c)).

a. Fit the elastic to your instep and pull the ends up and through the two slots in each of the cardboard shapes you have made. Then sew, or staple the ends of the elastic together and slide them round until the joined ends are underfoot.

b. Bend up and glue or staple the two cardboard flaps as shown.

c. Make two decorative shoe buckles out of silver-painted or foil-covered cardboard. See pages 112-115 for jewelry-making suggestions that are equally applicable to making buckles. Glue each buckle to and over the flaps of the cardboard disks you made.

d., e., f., g., h. and i. show different buckle designs. Make the bases out of metal screw-top bottle tops, scrap patent leather, plastic, oilcloth, canvas or foil-covered cardboard, or any other material firm enough to withstand use. Decorate these shapes with foil, colored paper, doilies, wallpaper scraps, and other found materials. Ribbon, satin fabric remnants, grosgrain, velvet, plaid and other decorative fabric can help you make the buckles in the shapes of valentines, easter eggs, or flowers. Diagram (i) shows a pom-pom shoe buckle. See page 41 for instructions on how to make it.

✂ Footwear

1. & 2. **Animal feet** (see also page 100 for paws). 1(a), (b) and (c) show different animal feet made out of decorated paper, cardboard, felt or cloth that can be fitted directly over ordinary shoes. Diagrams 2(a), (b) and (c) illustrate how to make them.

The duck foot (diagram (a)) can be made out of oilcloth, textured plastic material, felt or any other stiff fabric. The amphibian foot (diagram (b)) can be made out of felt, lamé, brocade, vinyl, or cardboard. The furry animal foot (diagram (c)) can be cut out of real or fake fur, toweling or any wooly material.

Design, fit and cut the pattern required for the front and back portions. Attach elastic to each matching set of feet at the places marked by crosses on the diagrams. Fit an additional strip of elastic round the instep under each shoe and attach to both sides of the foot covering, as described on page 102.

3. **Gathered shoes.** Diagram (a) shows the pattern for such a costume shoe. Use vinyl, oilcloth, or any other strong fabric. Gather the cloth with a strong needle and thread and sew on the strings by which to tie on the footwear as shown.

4. **Extended shoe** for a clown or medieval costume. Adapt the pattern shown in diagram (a) to suit the period or character of your costume. The shoe shown is rounded at the tip, but you may choose to make it pointed. Cut two identical shapes for each foot, the upper one made out of oilcloth or fabric, and the bottom half out of cardboard. Sew string to the upper portion as shown. Fit both halves to each shoe or foot, allowing ample room to slip them on and off after they are stapled and tied together.

5. **Papier mâché shoes.** Wooden clogs for a Dutch boy or girl, and similar large or heavy shoes can be made out of papier mâché and worn over ordinary shoes. Only a shell that fits over the upper portions of your shoes is required.

Design and cut the required front and back shapes out of cardboard (see diagrams (a), (b) and (c)). Staple edges together when the formed and bent shapes assume the required contours. You can add cardboard buckles and other decorative details to this armature. Then cover your shoes with clear plastic wrap or foil to protect them and place the cardboard armatures over them. See pages 62-63 for details on how to make and use papier mâché strips and mash with which to cover the armatures. When the papier mâché has dried thoroughly it can be painted. Diagram (d) shows how papier mâché clogs are worn over ordinary footwear. They can be removed after the play or party, restoring your shoes to their former state.

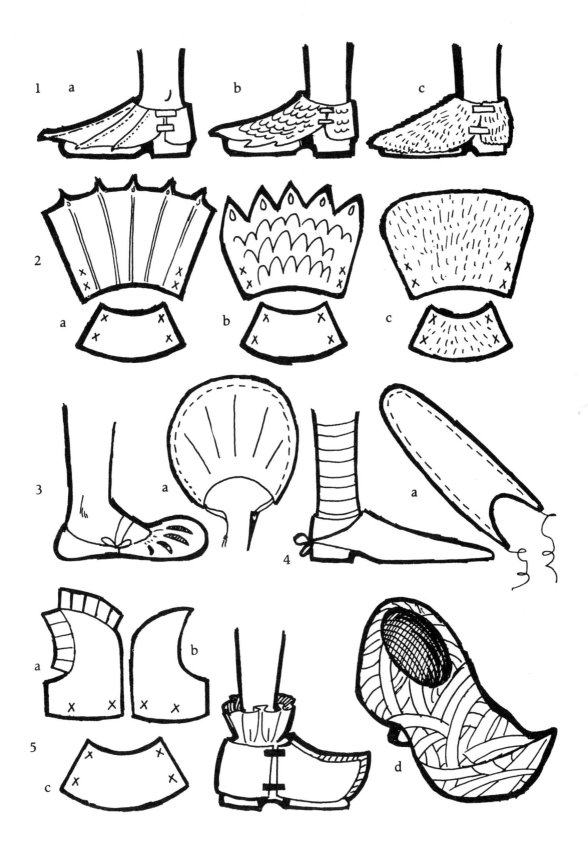

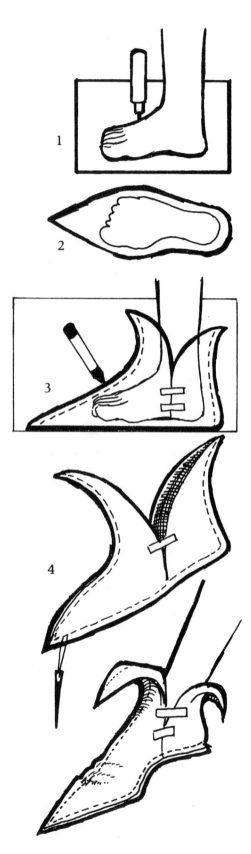

✂ Pointed shoes

1. **Measuring your foot.** Stand on a sheet of paper and mark the outlines of your bare feet accurately, using a crayon or felt marker. Be sure to leave enough room on the paper for adding to these outlines of your feet to include extensions that may be required for the shoe pattern.

2. Design the sole of the shoe and add whatever shape or extensions are needed, and add a 1 cm (½″) seam all around the pattern.

3. Stand a sheet of lightweight cardboard on its edge against one side of your leg, keeping your foot in place on the sole pattern you made. Draw the outline of your leg, as high as the shoe or boot is to be, onto the cardboard with a felt-tip pen. Mark the toe and heel to meet the sole you drew first. Place this sheet of cardboard flat on a table top. Then design the side-view of your shoe or boot in two parts — one to cover one half of the front of your foot, the other half way round the back of your heel. Duplicate these shapes and allow a 1 cm (½″) overlap where they meet on top of your foot and at the heel.

Once the cardboard pattern for one shoe is completed, transfer and trace each shape twice onto leather, vinyl, felt, or cloth. Be sure to cut out two matching pieces of each part of the toe uppers, and two for each heel — one set of four for each foot. Check whether you've left 1 cm (½″) extra where each shape attaches to any of the others, to serve as a seam. Then sew the toe portion of the uppers to the toe portion of the soles first, then heel to heel, before sewing the rest.

4. Sew the three sections — sole, toe, heel — together with heavy thread or thong. Sew an elastic strip on both sides of each foot covering at the side openings as shown, to allow you to slip them on and off.

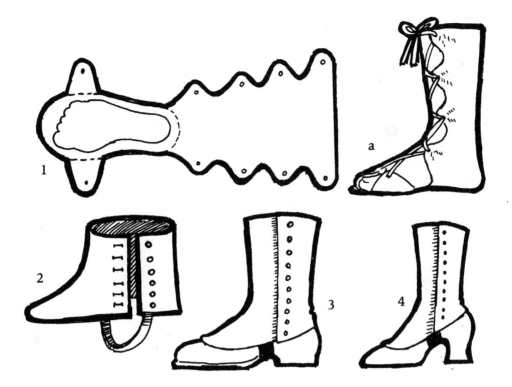

✂ Laced sandals and spats

1. Start with a sole pattern similar to that shown for the pointed shoes described on the opposite page. Different kinds of sandals require different additions and fastenings. A Greek sandal needs only an extended sole laced to the leg with leather thong or ribbons. The sandals and leggings shown here can be adapted to a variety of different periods and styles.

Design the sole and legging as shown. Bend the paper pattern up at the back of the leg and shape it. Flatten the pattern once more and add the flaps near the toes as indicated. Be sure to design the points that lace the shinbone of the leg so that they can be laced together through holes punched into each. Transfer the paper pattern to whatever final material is to be used; form it round the leg; and punch holes for lacing. Felt, leather, chamois, oilcloth, vinyl or upholstery fabric are best for such costume sandals and leggings. Use ribbon, string, leather or vinyl thong for lacing.

2. **Spats.** Fit the pattern round the ankles and over the shoes as before. Transfer the paper pattern to cloth, canvas, felt, oilcloth, vinyl, or leatherette. Punch hole, sew on buttons where shown, and add the elastic strip that fits under the instep of your regular shoe. Illustrations 3 and 4 show variations that convert ordinary shoes into high-button footwear worn during Victorian times and at the turn of this century.

✂ Stockings and socks

1, 2 & 3. Use a magic or fabric marker to draw onto any old socks or stockings. These are examples of some of the possible designs and effects. For best results, cut out a flat cardboard shape that matches that of the stocking. Fit the cardboard inside the stocking before drawing onto it. Otherwise the color may bleed through the top layer of fabric, staining the rest. Draw stripes, checks, fish scales, feathers and other designs onto the stockings. Marble effects, spotted and other irregular patterns can be tie-dyed into the fabric (see pages 126-127).

4. Abstract shapes, decorations, spots, animal toes and foot pads, can be ironed onto cotton or wool socks, but not onto synthetic materials.

✂ Leggings and pantaloons

Costuming for a Greek soldier at the turn of this century, a Tyrolean, an Eskimo or other characters requiring leg coverings that either tie or end below the knees.

1. **Pantaloons** can be made by sewing lace or other ruffled fabric on the lower legs of an old pair of pyjama pants. Or you can make a fabric tube that fits from below your knee to your ankle, sewn or stapled together, and cut from a length of material. Turn over the top of the tube and hem it, after running a length of elastic through the turned-over fabric. It will keep the tube in place just below the knee. Be sure not to make it too tight or it may restrict your circulation. Add layers of ruffles or lace as shown in diagram (a).

3. **Boot leggings.** See pages 52-53 for instructions on pattern making. Lay out two shapes, similar to that in 3, to fit each foot and leg. Each pair will make one legging. Be sure to add an extra centimeter (½") all round the pattern for the seam. Transfer the pattern to the fabric. Sew each set of two matching fabric shapes together on the wrong side. Turn them right side out and try them on. Then lace each foot and leg as shown in illustration 2.

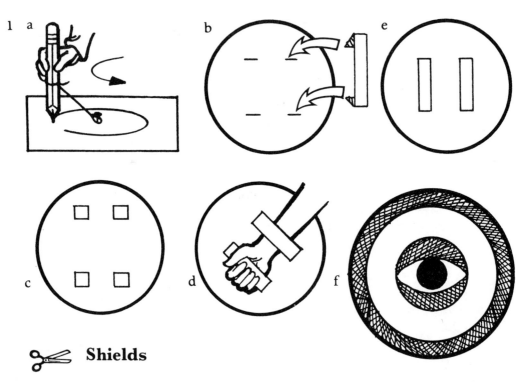

✂ Shields

African warriors, Greek soldiers, Roman centurions and European knights, among many other people of the past and present, use shields. While the shape of and designs on each may vary for different places and periods, the basic construction method is more or less the same.

1. The design shown here stems from ancient Greece. Make a paper pattern before transferring it to heavier material such as cardboard.

a. Draw a circle without compasses. Tape a large, square piece of wrapping paper to a table or the floor. Place a tack in its center. Tie a length of string to the tack, making a loose loop that turns easily when you move the string round. Tie a second loop at the other end of this string so that the length, from tack to the end of this second loop, is half the width of the circle you wish to draw. Insert a soft lead pencil or crayon into this second loop, point facing the paper. Maintain tension against the loop that holds the outer pencil and swing it all round the tack in the center to make the circle.

b. Use the pattern made, as shown in diagram (a), to cut out two identical cardboard disks. Place your hand and lower arm against one of these, as shown in diagram (d). Mark the spaces on this disk where hand grip and arm holder are to be attached as in diagram (b). Cut slots into all four marked spaces, each wide enough for ribbon to be passed through from one side to the other (diagram (b)). Cut and fit two ribbons as shown, slide their ends through the four holes, and glue or staple ends on the other side of the disk as shown in diagram (c). When glue is dry, glue the second disk on top of the first to hide the ends of the glued-on hand holds (c), and to strengthen the shield.

e. When turned over, the disk to which the hand holds are attached looks as shown.

f. Decorate the outside of the shield by painting it with poster colors, or by glueing designs onto it made out of colored paper, foil, leather, fabric or other found materials. Studs, nails, tacks, discarded hardware, old clock parts, buttons, plastic coffee can lids, among other materials, can be used imaginatively.

Shields need not be round. They can be oval, pointed at one or both ends and designed in a great variety of shapes. The construction method remains the same, especially in so far as arm and hand holds are concerned.

Spears, battle axes and other accessories can be made by cutting two identical shapes out of lightweight cardboard and stapling them round a broom stick or bamboo pole. Cover the whole head of spear or ax with foil. See pages 112-115 for jewelry-making instructions, and pages 62-69 for armor. The suggestions given there apply equally to shield- and weapon-making.

✂ Jewelry and body ornaments

Costume jewelry can be made out of any scrap, waste, or other material. Collect buttons, glitter, sequins, beans, bottle tops, cork, discarded game playing markers and counters, foil remnants, pieces of broken chain and mirror (be sure to file and sand sharp or pointed edges), pebbles or anything else that appeals to you. Keep whatever you collect in a separate container. Plastic or metal container lids and the plastic bubbles from packaging make useful bases for brooches and other ornaments. You'll also need plenty of cardboard, foil, colored paper, scissors, pliers, wire, string, glue, hammer and a nail, and a thick slab of wood as a working surface.

Design and prepare the base for whatever jewelry or ornaments you choose to make. Make your jewelry large. It's easier to work and looks more effective from a distance than small pieces. Place a plastic coffee can lid, tin can lid (with all edges filed and sanded smooth), or cut and shaped cardboard piece onto the wooden block and, using the hammer and a nail, make as many holes as required. Different ornaments require different fastenings to costume, neck, arm, leg, or each other. Neck, arm and leg ornaments can be made in hinged or laced together sections. Each part then needs as many holes as required to string them together.

See page 113 for details on how to use gold and silver paint. Be sure to paint lacing and hinges in the same color as the jewelry base. Once the paint is dry, glue beads and other findings to it in any design of your choice.

Costume jewelry can be made out of papier mâché. See pages 62-63 for instructions for making and using papier mâché strips and mash. The molded plastic, divisional trays of candy boxes and foil molds made for real jewelry can be filled with papier mâché mash which, when dried and painted, are effective costume accessories. They can be strung or adhered to one another and to plastic, metal, or cardboard costume jewelry bases, or pasted to belts, shields, armor, or clothing.

Be sure to look in jewelers' supply stores and at arts and crafts stores for earring findings, chain links and other inexpensive materials that will help you in your jewelry-making.

Painting jewelry

Silver paint needs a first undercoating of gray paint; golds needs an undercoating of Chinese red (orange) or cadmium red. It is nearly impossible to obtain a smooth, shiny gold or silver finish on painted surfaces. It's therefore best to create rough textures on jewelry that is to be painted in either color. Glue small pieces of doily, string, cheesecloth or crushed, dried leaves to whatever is to be painted. Cover the whole with the required undercoating. Let it dry thoroughly. Then use gold or silver paint, brushed on thickly and quickly, leaving parts of the undercoating exposed. The more irregularly the surfaces are painted, the richer and more antique-looking the finish will be.

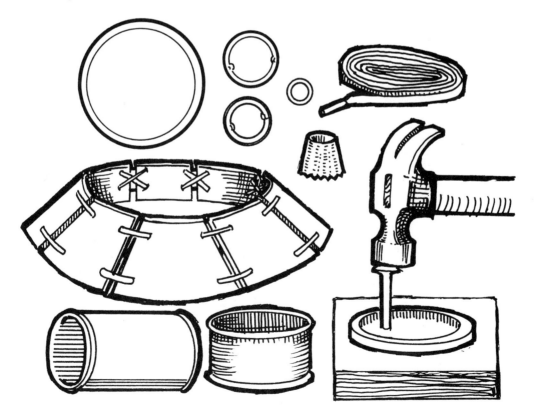

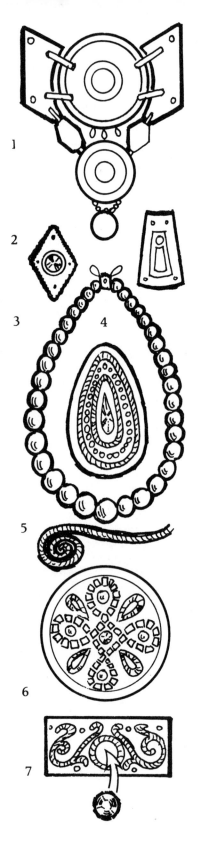

1

2

3

4

5

6

7

1. Combine different materials for unusual effects. Macaroni sections, dried seeds and beans can be painted and glued to larger shapes in imitation of pearls and jewels. They make rich-looking ornaments.

2. Three dimensional jewelry can be designed with layers of progressively smaller cardboard shapes, cut up and pasted on top of one another and then painted.

3. Papier mâché mash (page 65) can be used like clay to form beads for necklaces, belt decorations, earrings and pendants. Form them on a greased knitting needle or string. Remove them when dry and paint them.

4. Brooches can be made by pasting paper doilies or lace remnants to cardboard shapes, papier mâché formed or paper strip beads (see opposite page). These can be painted or decorated further with fake jewels or glitter.

5. Ordinary twine or string can ornament cardboard shapes. Dip the twine into paste and then twist the cord to form regular or asymmetrical designs. Paint when dry.

6. Eggshell mosaics make fancy costume jewelry. Spread glue on the surface of a cardboard, plastic or metal disk or shape. Press eggshell onto and into it, breaking the shell while adhering it. Paint each broken fragment in a different color after the glue has set.

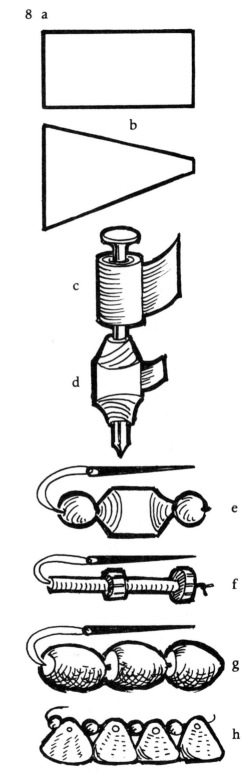

7. Fake jewels and broken mirror pieces can be set into large cardboard shapes by dipping lengths of twine into glue or paste and then adhering it onto the surface round each jewel. Remove the jewels before the glue dries. Paint the jewelry base. Then glue back each jewel.

8. **Paper beads.** Cut sheets of wallpaper samples into strips as shown in (a); the longer the strips are, the fatter the bead will be. Experiment with sizes. Large beads are usually the best. The rectangular strip shown in diagram (a) makes the long, tubular bead shown in diagram (c). The wedge-shaped strip shown in diagram (b) forms the oval bead shown in diagram (d).

Cover the "wrong" (unprinted) side of each strip with a thick coating of rubber cement, wallpaper paste, or mucilage. Then roll each bead over and around a knitting needle or pencil as shown in (c) and (d). If it tends to uncoil, fasten it with a rubber band. Allow all beads to dry thoroughly before removing them from the pencil. However, it's usually a good idea to move them back and forth from time to time while they dry to avoid their being glued to the pencil. String the dry beads with a large needle and heavy thread. Intersperse the rolled paper beads with macaroni sections, cork or other beads as shown in (e).

Acorns, pine cone sections and sea shells, left in their natural state or painted, can be strung as necklaces or used for other jewelry-making. See (f), (g) and (h).

1

2

3

4

5

6

✂ Extensions

A giraffe costume requires an extra long neck; a Santa Claus a fat stomach; a monster a hump back. These, and similar additions for a costume, require a sturdy harness strapped to your body. Diagram 6 shows such a harness that can be easily made and quickly adapted to many different purposes. Use drapery tape, canvas tape, or any sturdy fabric. You may need to change it to fit your particular costuming needs.

1. Use a long cardboard tube, or make one out of heavy wrapping paper, reinforced with papier mâché strips (see pages 62-63) or a length of bamboo tied or wired with pipe cleaners to the back of your harness to provide the base for the neck of the giraffe that, covered with fabric, will loom far above your head. The cloth covering should be designed to fit loosely for comfort and free movement. The coathanger wire frame attached to the harness serves as the giraffe's hindquarter. The pants for the front legs and the fake hind legs hung from the frame can be made out of old pyjama pants painted or dyed yellow, as is the fabric that covers the rest of the giraffe's body. Paint large, brown spots over all fabric portions and pyjama pant legs. The giraffe's head may be made of papier mâché over cardboard (pages 62-63) and painted to match the rest of the costume.

2. A coathanger wire frame holding up the angel's wings can be fastened to a harness similar to the one described and shown in 1 above. Cutting, twisting, and forming such heavy wire require a vise or wire forming jig, wire cutters and pliers. It also needs a good deal of strength. Ask father to help you. Be sure to cover the wire ends with friction or surgical tape to avoid possible injury. The wings themselves can be made of gauze, hung over and pasted to the wire frame. Oval or round fairy wings can be made in the same manner.

3. Any fat man, like Santa Claus, needs an old pillow or other padding attached to a harness worn back to front under the costume.

4. The Hunchback of Notre Dame needs similar stuffing attached to the back of the harness.

5. A Martian's "antennae" can be made out of wire, shaped as shown, to which several combs are taped firmly. Cover the ends of the wire with cork or rubber balls and paint the whole green. Wear by attaching the combs firmly to your hair or head covering.

Experiment with these ideas to turn yourself into whatever you choose to be. These are only some of the ways in which you can make yourself appear taller or fatter than you are. Some costume parts that extend far beyond your body may require counterweights for balance. For example, should the rear end of the giraffe costume shown in 1 above prove to be imbalanced, attach two small lead weights or a piping joint to the frame near the giraffe's tail.

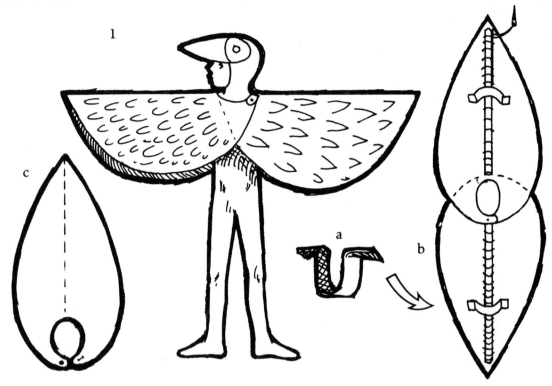

✂ Arm extensions

The following are instructions for turning arms into wings. The same method can be applied to any other arm extension, tentacles, or windmill sails for example.

1. **Arm wings.** They are designed in two separate, identical sections (diagram c), each of which buttons around the neck. Such a collar fastening allows each wing to be moved about freely, independent of the other, and without wrinkling. Make a paper pattern and adjust it to fit your arm length and neck girth. Then transfer the design to felt or other cloth. Sew slender strips of bamboo, lightweight wire, or feather boning into the underside of the wings, from shoulder to wing tip, to help keep their shape.
a. and b. Sew canvas straps or loops of elastic to the wrong side of the fabric of each wing so that your arms fit into them comfortably without restricting circulation. The neck opening can be made large enough to slip over your head. Or, if you prefer, one side of each can be cut through and each wing can then be attached to the neck with a button and buttonhole made at the ends of the openings.

✂ Fabric stiffeners

Feather boning can be sewn onto the fabric on the wrong side of any garment or costume part to stiffen small areas or to make them stand away from your body. It is usually sold in lengths embedded in cloth. This makes it easy to sew it onto fabric.

To make the bulging mouse costume (see illustration 2) or the Victorian skirt (see illustration 3) sew the feather boning to the fabric on the wrong side, in successive, parallel, circular strips, after the garment has been sewn. It is sometimes necessary to add short lengths of feather boning between such parallel strips, and at right angles to them, to obtain sufficient stiffness so that the costume retains the desired shape. Ask your mother for her help.

Some costumes require only short lengths of feather boning sewn into portions, at hems or ends to give them shape. In other instances you may wish to combine cardboard or papier mâché-formed portions of a costume with feather boning fabric adhered to them. For example a dragon's head might be made of papier mâché, while neck and body parts and the tail are made out of cloth, stiffened and reinforced with feather boning.

A bulky skirt or one that stands away from the body can be designed by first making a frame out of successively smaller rings of wire or feather boning, starting from the floor, each attached to the next with wire links or strips of heavy binding tape. Use binding tape for waistband. This frame can then be loosely covered with fabric, like a hoop skirt. For a gay nineties bustle effect, attach a piece of foam rubber to the back of a pair of swimming trunks.

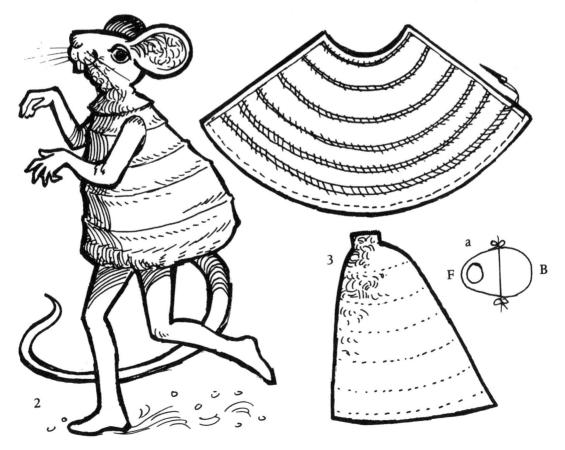

2

3

a

F   B

✂ Paper bag masks and costumes

Large paper shopping bags, produce, ice or laundry bags made of paper, can be adapted and decorated for instant wear as costumes. They require very little work. Plan cuts required for eye, arm, or other openings, so that a minimum of pasting or stapling is required. The fewer alterations you make, the longer your paper bag costume will last. **Do not use plastic bags. They are dangerous.**

Draw details on the paper bag mask or costume that identify the character or animal you choose to portray. Use magic marker or thick poster colors. Whiskers and other details can be drawn or pasted onto the costume. Keep in mind that paper bags are relatively fragile.

1. **Paper bag rabbit.** Use a large paper grocery or shopping bag (remove handles). Open the bag and stand it bottom side up. Cut an ear shape out of each side as shown in diagram (a), so that it hinges at the bottom (now the top) of the bag. Then make two short scissor cuts, one from each bottom edge of the bag towards its center (see diagram (a)) to make the ears face forward when each is stood up and creased (see diagram (b)). Glue or tape the ears upright with paper or cardboard supports or pipe cleaner wire glued to the back. Cut out the rabbit's face as shown in diagram (c) and use this opening to look out of your face mask.

2. **Raccoon, bear,** and other large animal paper bag masks and costumes can be made by cutting the ear shapes out of the back of the paper bag as shown in diagram (d), and folding them up. Trim the ears so that each matches the other. Cut a pointed flap into the front of the paper bag and bend it upward so that you can look out from under it. Cut holes into the sides for your arms as in diagram (e).

Cut the tail out of any other piece of paper (see pages 58-59, diagram (1)), or color it with crayons or magic markers and attach it to the rear bottom edge of the paper bag (see diagram (d)).

3. **Paper bag space helmet.** Cut a small shopping bag that fits your head as shown, so that it rests on your shoulders, upside down. Cut off the handles. Note the arches cut out of both sides of the open sides of the bag. Cut out the front window and paste cellophane or other transparent plastic wrapping material in place from the inside.

4. **Kachina or American Indian owl mask.** Choose and cut the paper bag as described in 3 for making a spaceman helmet, including the arched shoulder supports. Cut the triangular horns out of the sides and bend them up as shown. Cut and bend up the beak in front. Use this opening to allow you to look out of your mask. Paint eyes and traditional Indian symbols onto the paper bag costume.

5. **Paper poke hat.** Find a paper bag that is slightly larger than your head. Fold and roll up the open side of the bag until it fits your head snugly. Decorate this hat with doilies or pictures cut from magazines pasted to the paper bag, or with magic marker, after it is rolled up. Such paper poke hats are worn by people in the tropics to guard them against sunstroke.

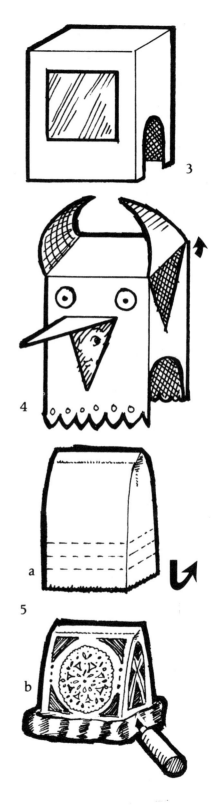

– 121 –

1a

1

b

2

2a

3

3b

Cardboard box costumes

1. **Cavalry man's horse.** A supermarket carton to which a horse's neck and head, made out of cardboard, have been glued or stapled. Cut out and fold cardboard shape; see diagram (b). Fold along dotted lines. Glue or staple to carton at shaded areas. Add ears at points marked X. Hang stuffed stockings, with boots painted on them, on either side; see diagram (a). For tail see page 58, diagram 1. Cut a hole into the top and bottom of the carton, large enough to step into and out of. For details on how to make the rider's costume see other pages of this book. Paint or decorate. Wear as shown here or in diagrams 4 and 4(a).

2. **Dune buggy.** Diagram (a) shows how to cut and bend the car's wheels out of the bottom flaps of the carton. Other details can be made out of sheets of board cut from a second carton and stapled, taped, or glued to the "car." Or details can be painted on. Strips of green and yellow raffia or yellow paper, attached to the bottom edges will give the impression that the "explorer" is travelling through tall grass. Wear as shown here or in diagrams 4 and 4(a).

3. **Ship.** Cut down the middle of the front panel of a long carton. Bend forward and flatten both halves of the cut-apart front panel. Then staple the sides (see diagram 3(b)) to form the pointed bow. Cut away excess portions. Tape or staple the loose bottom of the prow. The raised stern be made separately and taped or stapled to the "deck."

4. **Harness.** Use ribbon, belting or rope to make a harness that helps steady a cardboard box costume, enabling you to wear it in comfort. Cut slots into the top sides of the carton (see diagram (a) to which to attach the four ends of the ribbons.

5. **Skirt.** Staple or glue a gathered skirt to the box costume after it has been constructed and painted.

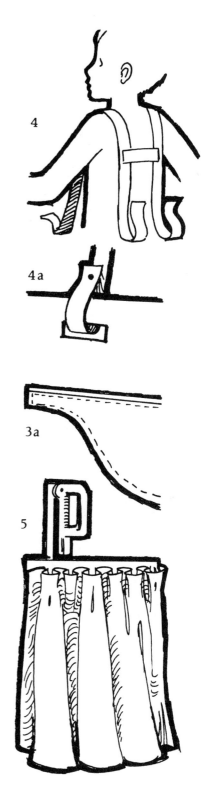

– 123 –

✂ Dyeing

Gather all fabric costume parts and accessories that are to be dyed the same color — shirt, pants, skirt, gloves, gown, and material remnants or swatches. It's easiest and best to dye all at the same time. No two batches of dye are ever exactly the same. Remember that synthetic fabrics may dye a different color from cotton or wool, or not take the dye at all.

Prepare the dye bath according to the instructions on the package. Dyeing in a washing machine is safest. Be sure to clean, rinse and run a strong solution of bleach through the washing machine after using it for dyeing.

For example, if you plan to make a dragon costume, as shown in the title page of this book, you might gather a tattered mattress cover, an old sweat shirt, a pair of worn-out mittens and a pillow case and dye the lot the same green in your family's washing machine. The mattress cover would then be converted into the dragon's hindquarter and tail and into his head covering. All other cited accessories and materials could go into making the rest of the costume.

When making costumes for a play, dye all garments and fabric to be used for costuming in two or three different dye baths in order to coordinate the color scheme for the production. Different details can be added in various colors, once the costumes are dyed and made. Unrelated and otherwise unlikely bits and pieces of cloth become harmonious when tied together by a basic color scheme. A book about color theory, or a color wheel, available in any art supply store or library, can help you decide which colors go together and complement one another, and which clash or provide contrast.

Graded intensity of color can be achieved in the following manner. Make a dye bath in a large pot or basin, according to the instructions on the package. Hang a large sheet, curtain or other length of fabric to be dyed on a clothes line or rack. Trail the bottom edge of the fabric into the dye bath. The color will "climb" up the package. Hang a large sheet, curtain or other length of fabric to be dyed on a clothes line or rack. Trail the bottom edge of the fabric into the dye bath. The color will "climb" up the fabric as it absorbs the moisture. The color will become progressively paler higher up, while the bottom edge will be dyed in the deepest hue of the color used. When the required shading and depth of tone are reached, remove the pot of dye and let the fabric dry on the line. Keep in mind, while dyeing, that the color will continue to climb even while the fabric is drying.

For a marbled effect, twist the fabric into a tight spiral before dipping it into the dye bath. Random dots and dashes of color can be made by placing the fabric flat on several layers of newspaper or wrapping paper. Then drip dye onto the material from a medicine dropper. Other effects can be achieved by dabbing dye onto the fabric with a sponge.

Be sure to wear rubber gloves while handling dyes and fabric that has just been dyed. Fabric dyes are toxic and can cause skin rashes. Once the dye has dried on the fabric it is safe for wear.

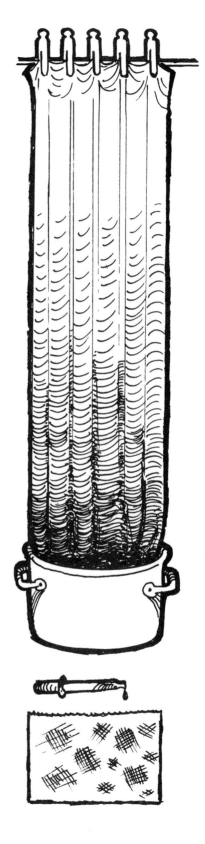

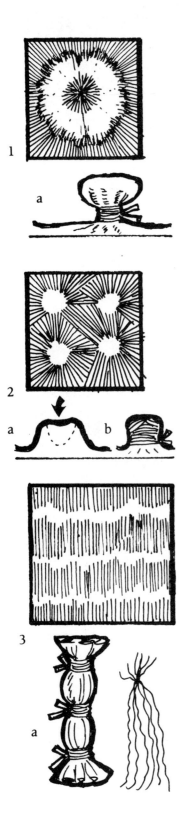

Tie dying and special effects

1. **White rings.** Wad together mushroom shaped tufts of fabric, as shown, as many as the number of rings desired to be dyed on that length. Wind string firmly round each tuft below the head of the mushroom. Once dipped into the dye bath (see pages 124-125), dried and untied, each segment will display one white ring surrounded by color. Be sure to keep the fabric tied until it has dried completely.

2. **White dots on colored background.** Gather up mushroom-shaped tufts as described in 1 above. Push a crater shape into the top of each mushroom with your finger as shown in diagram 2(a). Bind each tuft, including round the top so that the dye will not penetrate the indented crater. Dye as before and only remove the string after the fabric has dried.

3. **White stripes on colored background.** Gather the fabric carefully to form a long, tightly wound and compressed cylinder or roll. Bind it off as shown at regular and equidistant intervals (see diagram (a)). Then dye and dry as before.

4. **Marbled effect.** Gently form the fabric into a loose ball. Try to avoid folding any large

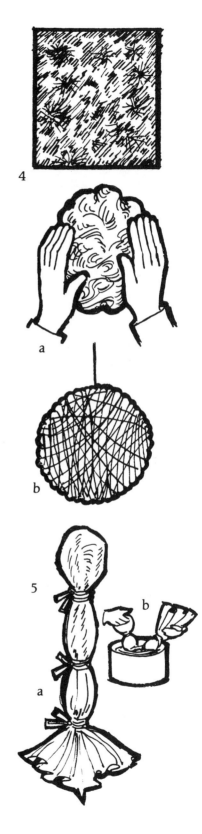

area of cloth inside this ball. Wind string tightly all round the ball in an irregular pattern, leaving spaces, no larger than a penny, between the strings. Dye and dry as before. Untie the ball. If the marbled effect is not uniform, re-tie the ball as before, making sure that all properly marbled areas are wound well inside it. Dye once more and let dry.

5. **Vari-colored concentric circles.** Lay a square of fabric flat on a table. Pick up the center with thumb and forefinger, letting the fabric drape loosely and naturally. Run your other hand over the hanging cloth so that the draped folds are more or less equally distributed all round. Tie off portions of the draped cloth as shown (see diagram (a)). Then prepare several dye baths, each of a different color. Dip each section of the tied cloth in a different colored dye bath (see diagram (b)). Let dry after all sections have been dyed. Remove the string. If you dip such a tied piece of fabric entirely into one single color, white, concentric circles will appear on the one color background after the cloth has been dried and untied.

Save all string used in tie-dying. It is useful for decorating costumes and accessories and for braiding into hair.

✂ Fabric panels

A garment or robe that requires a special panel which looks like rich brocade or embroidery, similar to the example shown here, can be prepared quickly with few materials. An old nightgown or discarded dress can be converted into a regal coronation costume.

Make a paper pattern for the area to be covered by the panel. Add 1 cm (½″) all round for the seam. Transfer the pattern to any discarded sheet, unbleached muslin or curtain fabric. Cut it according to the pattern and seam it all round. Then tape this fabric panel to newspaper or wrapping paper to keep it from wrinkling while you decorate it.

Tear or cut up tissue paper, dried leaves, doilies or fabric scraps. The torn or cut apart pieces should be very small and irregular and their quantity sufficient to cover the whole panel area. Then cover the fabric with rubber cement or acrylic medium. Drop the textured and cut apart fragments onto the glue-covered surfaces. Let dry thoroughly. Then paint the whole panel in gold or silver. See page 113 for under-painting instructions for gold and silver. When completely dry, sew the panel on the garment.

✂ Painting and stenciling on cloth

You can use textile paints to paint or stencil directly onto any natural fiber fabric — wool, cotton, silk, or felt. Synthetic fabrics require special paints. Whichever you use, experiment first on a small piece of the same fabric before applying the paint to the costume material itself. When decorating costumes for a stage production, paint or stencil shadows into the natural folds of draped fabric, using darker colors, and highlights on the outward curve of the folds by painting or stenciling them with light colors. Accentuate patched clothing, pockets and other details by outlining them with painted or stenciled-on prominent colors.

For any design that needs to be repeated, like fabric borders, heraldic signs, or a flower pattern for a dress, cut the required shape out of stencil paper, or wrapping paper saturated in vegetable oil, with the excess wiped off. Then use a stiff, short-haired stencil brush to dab and stipple color on cloth portions that show through the stencil.

Simple shapes cut into stencils can be combined and repeated to make more complex and multi-colored designs. Most fabric color paint jars or tubes include instructions for use with stencils.

✂ Exercises in make-believe

The costumes you make have two separate parts — one inside; the other outside. Other people see only your outside. But you can know, feel, imagine and be the character you choose to portray. A great actor doesn't need a costume to convince his audience. Professional actors spend a long time learning to fit themselves into roles that turn them into other people. The following are games you can play to help you learn to become an actor. They allow you to use your imagination, to place yourself in someone else's shoes, and to pretend, convincingly, to be who or whatever you decide to be. You may want to practice behind the closed door of your room, at first. Later, you'll want to act out these games with your family or friends.

Filling the bucket. Pretend that you have an empty bucket and a large bin filled with apples. Walk to the pretend bin, carrying your make-believe empty bucket. Fill it with apples and carry it away. Careful now! The bucket is heavy. How do you walk with a heavy bucket? Does it weigh you down on one side? Does it make you stagger? What is the position of your arms?

Now empty your make-believe bucket. How do you do that? How does it feel? Fill the bucket with feathers. Some get away and scatter all over the floor. Catch them. Pick up the rest. Don't leave any feathers about. Next, empty the bucket filled with feathers. Fill it up again with butterflies. How can you manage that? What happens? How would you act if you were given such a job?

Walking. Pretend that you are a robin. How does a robin walk? It doesn't. It hops. Keep your feet together and hop. Do you feel like a robin? Now make believe that you're a duck. Move all the furniture to one side of the room. Grab your ankles with both hands. Try waddling round. Is it difficult? Perhaps now you understand why ducks are always cross.

Next walk like a horse on two or four feet. Gallop round the room. Stomp on the floor, keeping the rhythm of hooves. It takes practice.

Now be a centipede. His feet look like ripples in your bath tub when he undulates, lifting one hundred legs in rapid succession. Can you do that? You haven't got a hundred legs, but you can pretend to be a centipede.

Now you're a wooden toy soldier. Walk with stiff, jerky arm and leg movements. A puppet moves differently. Be a puppet. Each of your limbs is being pulled in turn by strings attached to your knees and elbows.

Guessing. Now that you've practiced being and acting like someone or something else you are ready to play the following games with your friends. Act out a part and let them guess who you are and what you are doing.

Plant a seed in the ground, water it, and watch it grow. Act out what you are doing and what is happening by gesture alone, by how you move body and limbs without any props. Let your plant grow into a vegetable that you harvest, or a tree from which you pick fruit. Eat, sell, or give it away. Can they guess correctly? They should be able to if you act out your part properly.

Pretend to be going for a ride in a car, using a chair as your prop. Open the door. Get inside. Sit on the seat, start the engine and drive away. It starts to rain. Turn on your windshield wipers. A dog runs out into the street. What do you do? A policeman stops you for driving too fast. He gives you a summons. How do you act? Are your friends able to understand exactly what's happening?

Getting inside your part's skin. Pretend to be someone else. Think of a person or animal. You are asleep. Where and how do you sleep — in a nest, tree, canopied bed, or cradle? How does it feel to wake up and stretch? Open your eyes. What do you see — a branch, a cave, a hen house, or a castle?

Your eyes and ears are waking up also. What do you hear? What do you smell? What time of day is it? If you're an owl or a bat you wake up in the evening. What are you going to have for breakfast? If you are a chicken you start scratching for worms or seeds. If you're a lion you'll hunt for zebra or gazelle. If you're a king liveried servants will bring you food on gold trays.

Now pretend to spend the whole day as your new self. Where, how, and with what will you play or work? Who are your friends?

Once you can imagine yourself to be whoever you choose to be, you will have made the most important part of your costume. Then whatever costume you make for yourself will help convince, please or scare everyone else into believing that you really are who you pretend to be in your make-believe play at home, at a party, in a school play, or on Hallowe'en.

Bibliography

Allen, Judy, *Studio Vista Guide to Craft Suppliers*, London: Studio Vista, 1974

Arnold, Arnold, *Arts and Crafts for Children and Young People*, London: Macmillan, 1976

Appleton, LeRoy H., *American Indian Designs and Decorations*, New York: Dover, 1971

Bradley, Dennis, H., *The Eternal Masquerade*, London: T. Warner Laurie, 1926

Bruhn, Wolfgang; Tilke, Max, *A Pictorial History of Costume*, New York: Praeger, 1955

D'Assailly, Gisele, *Ages of Elegance*, London: MacDonald & Co., 1968

Fagg, William, *Tribes and Forms in African Art*, London: Methuen, 1965

Forkert, Otto Maurice, *Children's Theatre That Captures Its Audience*, Chicago: Coach House Press, 1962

Glubok, Shirley, *The Art of the Southwest Indians*, New York: Macmillan, 1971

Grimball, Elizabeth B.; Wells, Rhea, *Costuming a Play*, New York: Century & Co., 1925

Harris, Christie; Johnston, Moira, *Figleafing Through History*, New York: Atheneum, 1971

Hope, Thomas, *Costumes of the Greeks and Romans*, New York: Dover, 1972

Horn, Mary J., *The Second Skin*, Boston: Houghton Mifflin, 1968

Hughes, Talbot, *Dress Design*, London: Pitman & Sons Ltd., 1920

Jackson, Shiela, *Simple Stage Costumes and How To Make Them*, New York: Watson Guptil, 1968

Kehoe, Vincent, J. R., *The Technique of Film and Television Make-Up*, New York: Hastings House, 1958

Kyerematen, L.A., *The Panoply of Ghana*, New York: Praeger, 1964

Kybalova, Ludmila; Herbenova, Olga; Lamarova, Milena, *The Pictorial History of Fashion*, London: Paul Hamlyn, 1969

Laver, James, *Taste and Fashion*, New York: Dodd Mead & Co., 1938

——, *Costume*, New York: Hawthorne Books, 1964

Maile, Anne *Tie and Dye as a Present Day Craft*, New York: Ballantine Books, 1971

Moore, Sonia, *The Stanislavski System*, New York: Viking, 1965

Peters, Jean, Sutcliffe, Anna, *Making Costumes for School Plays*, London: P. T. Batsford Ltd., 1970

Pitseolak, *Pictures Out of My Life*, Montreal: Design Collaborative Books, 1971

Seidelman, James E.; Mintoyne, Grace, *Creating with Papier Mâché*, New York: Crowell-Collier Press, 1971

Spolin, Viola, *Improvisation for the Theater*, Chicago: Northwestern University Press, 1969

Wagner, Eduard; Drobna, Zoroslava; Durdik, Jan, *Tracht, Wehr, Waffen Des Spaeten Mittelalters, 1350-1450* (Arms and Armor), Prague: Artia, 1957

Knight's Pictorial Gallery of the Arts, Vol. 1, London: The London Printing and Publishing Co., Ltd., 1851 (wood cuts and engravings in this book stem from this source)

Index